one pot wonders

one pot wonders

Conrad Gallagher

with photographs by Gus Filgate

CB

CONTEMPORARY BOOKS

To Lauren, my daughter, with all my love

Thanks to Sophie, without whom this book

would never have been completed

Edited by Alexa Stace

Photography by Gus Filgate

Styling by Helen Trent

Designed by Mark Latter @ Vivid

Color Reproduction by Sang Choy

Production by Lorraine Baird & Sha Huxtable

First published in Great Britain in 2000 by

Kyle Cathie Limited

122 Arlington Road, London NW1 7HP

Library of Congress Cataloging-in-Publication Data

Gallagher, Conrad

One Pot Wonders/Conrad Gallagher;

  with photographs by Gus Filgate.

  p. cm.

"First Published in Great Britain in 2000"

T.p. verso.

Includes index.

ISBN: 0-8092-9445-1

1. Entrées (Cookery) 2. Casserole cookery. 3. Wok cookery. I. Title.

TX740.G34 2001

641.8–dc21   00-46601

Published by Contemporary Books

A division of NTC/Contemporary Publishing Group, Inc.

4255 West Touhy Avenue, Lincolnwood (Chicago),

  Illinois 60712-1975 U.S.A.

Printed in Singapore

International Standard Book Number: 0809294451

10 9 8 7 6 5 4 3 2 1

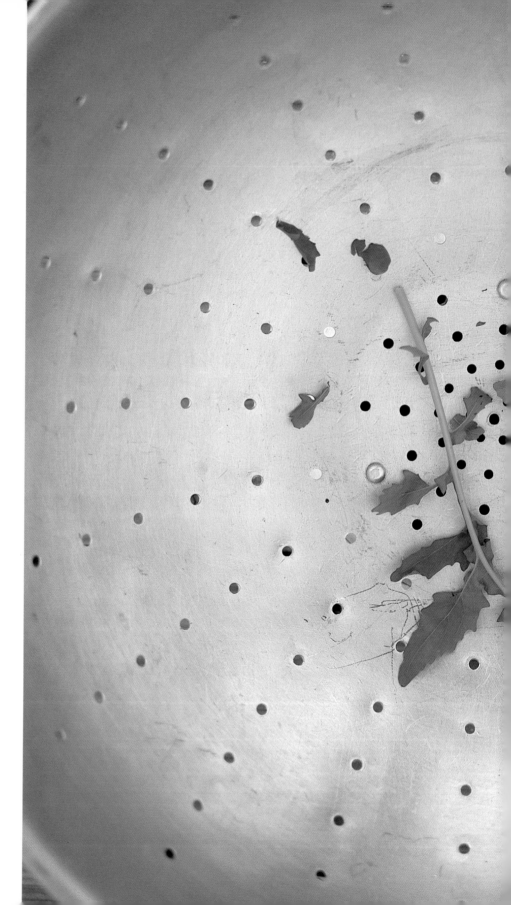

contents

introduction

The idea for this book is a simple one. The recipes are designed so that with a little thought and preparation – and sometimes even with none at all – they can be cooked using just one pan. In many cases you can even serve them in the pan.

The reasoning behind this is simple. By imposing the one-pan discipline I forced myself to simplify some of the more complicated dishes we serve in our restaurants. I feel that this makes the dishes less intimidating to people who would like to try something different, but who do not necessarily possess a huge kitchen and a massive arsenal of cookware. Plus it saves on the dish washing. After all, when you are cooking at home for friends and family, no matter how much you enjoy it, you should aim to spend more time eating the food than you do cooking it – or clearing up afterwards. It is an essential part of my philosophy that food can be sophisticated, yet simple; that meals can be classy, without being complicated. In our restaurants we are blessed with a large staff, lots of space and an impressive array of equipment. And even when we are under immense pressure we still have plenty of time to devote to preparation. At home you may not have any of that, but just because you are short of time, space, or equipment doesn't mean that you can't produce great-tasting, good-looking food which is fun to cook and enjoyable to eat.

I've always believed that food – whether eating out in a restaurant or at home – should be an enjoyable experience. When you cook at home there's a reason why it's called entertaining – it should be! I hope that *One Pot Wonders* will help with that, and that it encourages you to experiment further in your own kitchen.

RESTAURANT

PEACOCK

ALLEY

saucepan

In my restaurants I always use copper-lined saucepans. Copper conducts heat evenly and ensures that ingredients do not get scorched at high temperature and during quick cooking. Copper pans are expensive, but they are a good investment if you do cook a lot, as they can last for years if well maintained. Otherwise stainless steel saucepans are readily available and are excellent for one-pot cooking.

In the South of France they serve this for breakfast during the asparagus festival. Slices of black truffle add a luxurious touch, and diced truffle gives the hollandaise sauce a heavenly, unforgettable aroma.

asparagus with poached egg
and truffle hollandaise

you will need

8 quail eggs

1 tbsp. wine vinegar

16 asparagus spears, blanched

2 tbsp. melted butter

16 arugula leaves (optional)

8 thin slices of black truffle (optional)

Selection of chopped herbs
for garnishing

1 tomato, peeled, seeded and chopped

TRUFFLE HOLLANDAISE

1 shallot, finely diced

¼ cup white wine

1 tbsp. chopped fresh thyme

4 egg yolks

2 sticks (1 cup) butter, diced

⅛ oz. black truffle, finely diced

Serves 4

First make the hollandaise sauce. Place the shallot, white wine, and thyme in a medium-sized pan. Bring to a boil and cook until reduced by half. Remove from heat and transfer to a bowl. Rinse out the pan, fill with water, and bring to a boil.

Add the egg yolks to the bowl and whisk, then place the bowl in the pan of boiling water. Remove the pan from the heat and gradually add the diced butter, whisking continuously. Each time, allow the butter to melt and the sauce to thicken before adding more. If you think the sauce is going to separate, take the bowl out of the pan and add a few teaspoons of cold water to the sauce. Continue until all the butter has been added. Add the diced truffle and keep warm in a water bath until ready to use.

Bring the water back to a boil and preheat the broiler. Add the vinegar to the pan and poach the eggs until soft, then transfer to a bowl of cold water until ready to use.

Place the asparagus under the broiler and brush with the butter. Broil lightly for 1 minute on each side, then arrange on a serving dish on a bed of arugula, if using. Reheat the eggs in a bowl of boiling water, then drain. Arrange the slices of truffle on top of the asparagus, and top each slice with a quail egg. Drizzle with the hollandaise sauce, and garnish with a selection of fresh herbs and chopped tomato.

I first sampled morels in the West of Ireland in 1985, roasted with garlic and parsley, and I can still remember the taste. Wanting that taste becomes a craving, like waiting for the truffle season, and my order is always in early, so that morels are sure to be on the menu while they are in season.

peas & morels

with fried quail eggs

you will need

2lbs. fresh shelled peas

Salt and freshly ground
   black pepper

3 tbsp. olive oil

½ stick (¼ cup) butter

6 shallots, diced

2 tsp. chopped rosemary

2 tsp. chopped thyme

2 cloves garlic, crushed

⅓lb. morels, stems trimmed

1¼ cups Chicken Stock (see page 153)

⅔ cup heavy cream

½ cup Beef Jus (see page 157)

4 quail eggs

Flat-leaf parsley sprigs, for garnishing

Serves 4

Cook the peas in a pan of boiling salted water for 2–3 minutes. Refresh in cold water, drain, pat dry, and set aside. Rinse out the pan.

Place the olive oil and 3 tablespoons of the butter in the pan over medium heat. Add the shallots, rosemary, thyme, and garlic, and sauté for 3–4 minutes. Add the peas, morels, chicken stock, cream, and beef jus to the pan, and cook for another 2–3 minutes.

Transfer the mixture to a large bowl and keep warm. Rinse out the pan. Melt the remaining butter in the pan and lightly fry the quail eggs. Serve the peas and morels with the eggs on top and garnish with sprigs of parsley.

Dublin Bay prawns, also known as scampi, are the best, and the freshest. The prawn shells are first sautéed in olive oil with garlic and shallots, then simmered in chicken stock, giving an added depth of flavor to the rich, creamy pasta sauce.

linguine

with dublin bay prawns

Cook the linguine in a pan of boiling salted water for 8 minutes, or until al dente. Drain, refresh in cold water, and drain again. Rinse out the pan.

Heat 1 tablespoon of the olive oil in the pan until it is smoking. Add the prawns and sauté for 1 minute on each side. Remove from the pan and set aside.

Heat the remaining oil in the pan until it is smoking. Add the prawn shells, garlic, and shallots, and sauté for 3 minutes. Add the tomato paste and chicken stock, bring to a boil, and simmer until reduced by half. Add the cream and simmer for 5 minutes. Pour the sauce through a fine sieve and adjust the seasoning.

Return the sauce to the pan and mix in the linguine, peas, tarragon, and prawns. Heat gently to warm through, tossing well. Season to taste and serve.

you will need

7oz. dried linguine

2 tbsp. olive oil

20 Dublin Bay prawns, shelled and deveined, shells reserved

1 clove garlic, crushed

2 shallots, finely chopped

2 tbsp. tomato paste

2½ cups Chicken Stock (see page 153)

2½ cups heavy cream

Salt and freshly ground black pepper

½ cup garden fresh peas, blanched

1 tbsp. tarragon leaves

Serves 4

garlic mash

Place the potatoes in a pan of salted water. Bring to a boil, reduce the heat, and cook for 20 minutes, or until the potatoes are tender. Drain, mash, and transfer to a bowl. Rinse out the pan.

Place the cream and garlic in the pan and cook gently until reduced by a quarter. Strain into a bowl, add the butter, and allow it to melt. Add the cream mixture to the potatoes and mix well. Reheat and season if necessary.

you will need

8–12 medium potatoes, peeled and cubed

Salt

1 cup heavy cream

3 cloves garlic, lightly crushed

1 stick (½ cup) butter

Serves 4

Heavenly Italian scents and flavors combine to magnificent effect in this simple but impressive pasta recipe.

pappardelle with prosciutto, *arugula, pine nuts, and parmesan*

you will need

9oz. dried pappardelle or other dried egg noodles

Salt and freshly ground black pepper

3 tbsp. Basil Pesto (see page 155)

3oz. (about ¾ cup) prosciutto, diced

½ cup pine nuts

1¾ cups grated Parmesan

1 large handful arugula

Serves 4

Cook the pappardelle in a large pan of boiling salted water until al dente, then drain well and return to the pan over a low heat. Add the pesto and mix into the pappardelle. Add the prosciutto, pine nuts, and Parmesan, and toss well.

Stir in the arugula until just wilted, adjust the seasoning, and serve immediately.

Flavored risottos are very fashionable, using everything from squid ink to fresh herbs, but this is my favorite. In the States I always loved the pumpkin season, and this risotto is the perfect dish for an autumnal flavor.

pumpkin risotto

with trompettes de mort and pancetta

you will need

THE RISOTTO

2 tbsp. butter

2 shallots, finely diced

1 clove garlic, crushed

1 tsp. thyme

1¼ cups arborio rice

1 cup white wine

1 quart hot Vegetable Stock (see page 153)

½ cup heavy cream

1 cup grated Parmesan

2oz. (about ¾ cup) pancetta, thinly sliced

¼lb. trompettes de mort (black chanterelles) sautéed in ½ stick (¼ cup) butter

¼ cup mascarpone

1 tbsp. diced red pepper for garnishing

PUMPKIN PURÉE

2 small pumpkins, peeled, seeded, and diced

2 cloves garlic, crushed

¼ cup olive oil

3 sprigs thyme

Serves 4

For the purée, preheat the oven to 400°F. Place the pumpkin in a heavy, ovenproof pan along with the garlic, olive oil, and thyme. Roast for 30 minutes, then remove from the oven and let cool. Transfer to a food processor, blend until smooth, then push through a fine sieve into a bowl. Rinse out the pan.

For the risotto, melt the butter in the pan. Add the shallots, garlic, and thyme, and cover and sweat over medium heat until soft. Add the rice and white wine. Cover and sweat for about 2 minutes on a medium heat, then uncover and let it reduce until almost dry. Gradually add the vegetable stock to the rice, stirring continuously after each addition until all the stock has been absorbed and the rice is tender.

Mix the cream and the Parmesan into the risotto, then mix in the pumpkin purée. Serve in bowls and arrange the pancetta and trompettes de mort on top. Add a spoonful of mascarpone to each serving, and garnish with the diced pepper.

The secret of making perfect risotto is to use good-quality rice and a well-flavored stock. It is important to add the hot stock gradually, stirring well after each addition until the liquid is absorbed.

gorgonzola
and red onion risotto

you will need

2 tbsp. olive oil

2 large shallots, diced

1 large red onion, finely diced

½ cup dry white wine

1¼ cups risotto rice, such as arborio

1 tsp. thyme

1 quart hot Chicken Stock (see page 153)

1 tbsp. heavy cream

1 tbsp. Gorgonzola

2 tbsp. butter

Salt and freshly ground black pepper

1 tbsp. grated Parmesan

Serves 4

Heat the oil in a heavy pan over medium heat. Add the shallots and red onion, cover, and sweat for 3–4 minutes until soft. Add the white wine and simmer until reduced by half. Bring to a boil and add the rice and thyme.

Start adding the hot stock gradually, stirring after each addition until all the liquid has been absorbed. When all of the stock has been absorbed and the rice is tender, stir in the cream, Gorgonzola, and butter. Season with salt and pepper and sprinkle with the grated Parmesan before serving.

Fresh spring vegetables lend their name to this delicately flavored risotto, a perfect vehicle for serving up the first asparagus of the season.

risotto primavera

Melt half of the butter, along with the olive oil, in a heavy pan over medium heat. Add the garlic and shallot, and sauté for 3–4 minutes or until soft.

you will need

1 stick (½ cup) butter

1 tbsp. olive oil

1 clove garlic, crushed

1 shallot, finely diced

1¼ cups arborio or other risotto rice

1 quart hot Vegetable Stock (see page 153)

¼lb. (2 large handfuls) baby spinach

1 cup fresh peas, blanched until tender

12 asparagus spears, blanched until tender and cut into 1-inch pieces

⅓ cup white wine

Salt and freshly ground black pepper

2 tbsp. heavy cream

½ cup parsley, chopped

1¾ cups grated Parmesan

Serves 4

Add the rice, stir well, and cook for 2 minutes. Start adding the stock gradually, stirring continuously after each addition until the liquid is absorbed. When most of the liquid has been absorbed and the rice is tender, add the vegetables and white wine, mix well, and cook for 1 minute.

Remove from heat, season with salt and pepper, and add the remaining butter, the cream, chopped parsley, and Parmesan. Mix well and serve at once.

Orzo are small pasta shapes which look like grains of rice. They make an attractive presentation in this one-pot dish which would be ideal for a quick lunch or supper.

orzo with feta,

mint and plum tomatoes

Cook the orzo in boiling salted water until al dente, then drain, rinse under cold water, and drain again thoroughly.

Mix in the remaining ingredients, season well, and serve garnished with fresh mint or arugula and sundried tomatoes.

you will need

8oz. orzo

Salt and freshly ground black pepper

¼ cups extra virgin olive oil

Juice of 2 lemons

2 tbsp. finely chopped mint

¼lb. (about 2 cups) feta cheese, diced

4 plum tomatoes, finely diced

⅔ cup good quality pitted black olives

Mint or arugula and sun-dried tomatoes for garnishing

Serves 4

Polenta cakes, cut into circles with a cookie cutter, make an attractive accompaniment to fish or poultry. They need to be well flavored, so add a good selection of fresh, chopped herbs.

polenta cake with goat cheese
and herbs

Heat the milk, cream, butter, shallots, and garlic together in a heavy pan.
Bring to a boil, then reduce the heat to a simmer. Slowly add the polenta in a thin stream, stirring constantly with a wooden spoon. Continue to simmer on the lowest heat, stirring frequently, until the mixture is thick and comes away from the sides of the pan. The polenta will lose its corn taste after about 45 minutes.

Stir in the goat cheese and herbs, and cook for 1–2 minutes. When it's cooled, spread it out to about ½-inch thick on a flat tray, and let it set. When cold, cut out circles using a 2½-inch cookie cutter. To serve, reheat in the oven, shallow-fry in olive oil, or broil on both sides until golden.

you will need

2 cups milk

⅔ cup heavy cream

1 tbsp. butter

2 shallots, finely chopped or,
  if unavailable, 1 small mild onion

1 garlic clove, crushed

3 cups polenta (corn meal)

¼lb. goat cheese

Handful of herbs, such as basil,
  chives, cilantro, chervil,
  finely chopped.

Serves 4

This dish is true fusion. Harissa, a hot sauce which comes from North Africa, often served with couscous, is teamed with a spicy Indian masala sauce to give zest to these unusual medallions. If kangaroo is difficult to find, substitute with a nice piece of pork.

kangaroo medallions

with harissa and spicy masala sauce

To make the sauce, dry-roast the shrimp paste in a large, heavy pan over medium heat. Add the oils and fry the onion, garlic, ginger, galangal, chiles, turmeric, and cilantro roots. Add the dried shrimp and spices. Stir in the tomato paste, coconut cream, and palm sugar, and cook on gentle heat until the mixture starts to bubble. Add the stock, bring to a boil, then simmer for 1 hour until reduced by at least half. Skim off any excess oil and scum, remove from heat and pass through a sieve into a bowl. Add the fish sauce and season to taste. Rinse out the pan.

Mix the pepper and coriander and sprinkle them over the medallions, then brush with olive oil. Heat the pan until very hot and sear the meat for about 2–3 minutes on each side, depending on how rare you like it. Spoon some sauce around each plate, place a medallion in the center, and add a teaspoon of harissa on top of the meat. Serve with fresh vegetables.

you will need

1 tsp. black peppercorns, ground

1 tsp. coriander seeds, ground

4 x 5oz. kangaroo medallions

Olive oil

6 tsp. harissa

Fresh vegetables for serving

SPICY MASALA SAUCE

2 tsp. shrimp paste

5 tbsp. vegetable oil

2 tbsp. sesame oil

1 onion, finely chopped

4 cloves garlic, finely chopped

1 tbsp. finely chopped ginger root

2 slices galangal, finely chopped

5 red chiles, seeded and

    finely chopped

2 slices of turmeric, finely chopped

4 cilantro roots, crushed

2 tsp. dried shrimps, roasted

    and ground

1 tsp. sichuan peppercorns,

    ground

1 tsp. cumin seeds, ground

2 tsp. coriander seeds, ground

1 tsp. turmeric powder

Pinch of freshly grated nutmeg

8 fresh curry leaves (available from

    Asian food stores)

1 stick cinnamon

½ cup tomato paste

⅔ cup coconut cream

2oz. palm sugar (jaggery), shaved

    (available from Asian food stores)

5 cups Beef Stock (see page 153)

2 tbsp. fish sauce (available from

    Asian food stores)

Serves 4

The combination of parmesan and coconut is unusual, but it works very well in this simple but effective pasta dish.

fettuccine with squash,

scallions, parmesan, and coconut

Preheat the oven to 350°. Roast the squash in the preheated oven for 15 minutes. Remove from the oven and let it cool, then peel, seed, and cut it into ½ inch cubes.

you will need

1 medium butternut squash

1 bunch scallions, sliced

Salt and freshly ground black pepper

13oz. dried fettuccine

2 tbsp. olive oil

1 x 13oz. can of coconut cream

½ cup grated coconut

½ cup grated Parmesan

Serves 4

Blanch the onions in a large pot of boiling water for 1 minute. Refresh under cold water and pat dry. Salt the boiling water, add the pasta, and cook until al dente. Drain and set aside.

Rinse out the pot, then heat the olive oil over medium heat. Add the squash and scallions, cover, and sweat for 3–4 minutes. Add the coconut cream and simmer for 5 minutes. Stir in the grated coconut, season to taste, and remove from heat. Add the pasta, toss well to heat through, and serve sprinkled with grated Parmesan.

deep pot

It would be difficult to cook these recipes without a deep pot.

As you will see, with this pot you can steam, make soup, and prepare pasta. You will need a steaming

basket, and when you buy a deep pot it often comes with one. The pan should be high quality,

stainless steel. Size is up to you, but I recommend a big pot, as you could prepare meals for large

numbers of people in it.

I adore pumpkin, but butternut squash makes a lovely alternative. The cumin cream gives this soup a wonderfully smooth, nutty flavor.

butternut squash soup

with cumin cream

To make the cumin cream, pour the cream into a bowl and stir in the lemon juice. Fold in the ground cumin, and season with salt and pepper.

you will need

2lbs. butternut squash, peeled, and cut into thick chunks

1 quart Chicken Stock (see page 153)

1¼ cups crème fraîche or, if unavailable, a mixture of heavy cream and sour cream

2 tbsp. butter

Salt and freshly ground black peppeer

Several chives, cut into 1-inch lengths

CUMIN CREAM

2 cups heavy cream

Juice of 2 lemons

¾ cup ground cumin

Serves 4

Place the squash and the stock in a large pot over high heat. Bring to a boil, then reduce the heat and simmer for 20 minutes. Remove from heat and let the mixture cool, then purée in a blender until smooth

Return the purée to the pot over medium heat. Stir in the crème fraîche, cumin cream, butter, and salt and pepper. Stir until heated through, adding more seasoning if necessary. Serve garnished with the chives.

This is a classic Thai dish – hot, spicy and sweet. It is very popular, but it is difficult to find it cooked properly. This is how it should be done.

thai chicken & coconut soup

with shiitake mushrooms

Heat 2 tablespoons of the olive oil, along with the butter, in a large pot over low heat. Add the lemon grass, shallots, garlic, scallions, thyme, and rosemary, and cover and sweat for 3–4 minutes. Add the peanut butter and stir until smooth.

Pour in the coconut milk, bring to a boil, and simmer until reduced by half. Add the chicken stock and wine, and return to a boil, then pour in the cream. Remove from heat and let it cool. Purée the soup in a food processor, then pass through a fine sieve.

Rinse the pot, then heat the remaining olive oil over low heat. Add the shiitake mushrooms, chiles, and bean sprouts. Cover and sweat for 3–4 minutes. Add the soup and chicken breast and heat through gently.

Serve sprinkled with chopped cilantro.

you will need

½ cup olive oil

½ stick (¼ cup) butter

2 stalks lemon grass, chopped

3 shallots, finely chopped

2 cloves garlic, crushed

1 bunch scallions, finely chopped

1 tbsp. thyme leaves

1 tbsp. rosemary leaves

1 tsp. peanut butter

1 cup coconut milk

2½ cups Chicken Stock (see page 153)

½ cup white wine

½ cup heavy cream

⅓lb. fresh shiitake mushrooms, chopped (about 2⅓ cup)

2 chiles, seeded and finely diced

1 cup bean sprouts

4 chicken breasts, skinned, poached, and diced

Chopped cilantro, for garnishing

Serves 4

This is a peasant dish done in gourmet style to make it rich and creamy, with the subtle, spicy flavors of Southeast Asia.

john dory

with coconut and curry

you will need

¼ cup olive oil

3oz. lemon grass, finely chopped

10 shallots, sliced

3 cloves garlic, sliced

3 sprigs thyme

5 curry leaves

1-inch ginger root, peeled and grated

1 stick (½ cup) butter

2 tbsp. curry powder

3 tbsp. turmeric

1½ quarts Chicken Stock (see page 153)

2 cups heavy cream

1 cup coconut milk

2 tbsp. coconut cream

2lbs. John Dory fillets, skinned

Salt and freshly ground black pepper

shredded lettuce, for serving

Chiles, whole and sliced, for garnishing

Serves 6

Place the olive oil in a large pot over low heat. Add the lemon grass, shallots, garlic, thyme, curry leaves, and ginger, and cover and sweat for 5 minutes. Stir in the butter, curry powder, and turmeric. Add the chicken stock and cream, and bring to a boil. Simmer for 10 minutes then add the coconut milk and coconut cream.

Press the soup through a fine chinois sieve or cheesecloth, then reheat and add the fish fillets. Cover and simmer gently for 3–5 minutes or until the fish is cooked. Season to taste and serve garnished with shredded lettuce and chiles.

For those who adore shellfish, this is quick, simple – and irresistible.
The sharp tang of watercress and lime is a delightful surprise.

mussels & clams

with lime and watercress

you will need

½ cup white wine

48 small mussels, scrubbed and rinsed, with
beards removed

24 small clams, rinsed

⅛ cup olive oil

Zest and juice of 1 lime

1 carrot, diced

1 zucchini, diced

2 large shallots, diced

1 fennel bulb, diced

1 bunch watercress or, if unavailable, baby
spinach leaves

Salt and freshly ground black pepper

Serves 4

Pour the white wine into a large pot and add the mussels and clams. Cover and cook on high heat for about 5 minutes until the shells have opened. Drain the mussels and clams, reserving the liquid. Shell the mussels and clams, discarding any that remain closed.

Return the liquid to the pot. Bring to a boil and reduce by half. Mix in the olive oil, lime zest and juice. Add the vegetables, reduce the heat, and simmer for about 5 minutes, or until the vegetables are tender.

Add the watercress, mussels, and clams, and reheat gently. Season to taste and serve immediately.

Mussels are child's play to cook. Try this oriental take on the traditional mussels in cream sauce.

steamed mussels

with lemon grass, ginger, and coconut

you will need

2 tbsp. olive oil

3 cloves garlic, crushed

4 shallots, finely chopped

2 stalks lemon grass

2-inch ginger root, peeled and finely chopped

½lb. (about 2½ cups) leeks, chopped

1 cup carrots, chopped

½lb. (about 2½ cups) celery, chopped

1 sprig thyme

1 sprig rosemary

2lbs. mussels, scrubbed and rinsed, with beards removed

1¼ cups white wine

1 quart fish stock

⅓ cup coconut milk

½ cup light cream

Salt and freshly ground black pepper

2 tbsp. chopped cilantro

Serves 4

Heat the olive oil in a large pot over gentle heat. Add the garlic, shallots, lemon grass, ginger, leeks, carrots, and celery. Cover and sweat for 5–6 minutes or until soft. Add the thyme and rosemary and transfer to a bowl. Rinse out the pot.

Put the mussels, white wine, and fish stock in the pot over high heat. Cover and steam for about 5 minutes or until the mussels open. Remove the mussels with a slotted spoon and place in a large serving dish, discarding any mussels that have not opened.

Add the vegetables to the cooking liquid, bring to a boil, and cook until reduced by half. Stir in the coconut milk and cream, and adjust the seasoning. Add the chopped cilantro, and pour the sauce over the mussels.

Chiles and garlic give these mussels a real punch. Serve with crusty French or the basil bread (see page 157).

steamed mussels

with garlic, cilantro, and chiles

Heat the olive oil in a pot over low heat. Add the garlic, chiles, shallots, ginger, leeks, and celery. Cover and sweat for 5–6 minutes or until soft. Add the thyme and rosemary and transfer to a bowl. Rinse out the pot.

Place the mussels, white wine, and fish stock in the pot over high heat. Cover and steam for about 5 minutes, or until the mussels open. Remove the mussels with a slotted spoon and place in a serving dish, discarding any that have not opened.

Add the vegetables to the pot. Bring to a boil and cook until reduced by half. Remove from the heat, stir in the cream, and adjust the seasoning. Add the chopped herbs, pour the mixture over the mussels, and serve.

you will need

2 tbsp. olive oil

4 cloves garlic, crushed

2 chiles, seeded and sliced

4 shallots, chopped

1oz. ginger root (about ½-inch piece), peeled and chopped

3 leeks, chopped (about 3-4 cups)

1 stalk of celery, chopped

1 sprig thyme

1 sprig rosemary

2lbs. mussels, scrubbed and rinsed, with beards removed

1¼ cups white wine

1 quart fish stock

½ cup heavy cream

Salt and freshly ground black pepper

1 cup chopped cilantro

1 cup chopped flat-leaf parsley

Serves 4

gnocchi

These traditional Italian dumplings make a wonderful accompaniment to broiled meats or pasta with sauces.

Place the potatoes in a bowl and make a well in the center. Add the cornmeal and egg yolks and mix into a dough, then mix in the flour. Season with salt and pepper and mix in the chives and thyme.

Roll the dough into a sausage shape, then cut into 1-inch pieces. Bring a large pot of water to a boil. Add the gnocchi and simmer for 1 minute. They will float to the top when ready. Remove with a slotted spoon and drain on paper towels.

you will need

2lbs. hot mashed potatoes

1 tbsp. cornmeal

5 egg yolks

3 tbsp. flour

Salt and freshly ground black pepper

2 tbsp. chopped chives

1 tsp. finely chopped thyme

Serves 4

For a really spectacular presentation, use deep-fried strips of eggplant skin to make a flamboyant garnish, as illustrated.

crab salad

with avocado cream

To make the avocado cream, blend the avocado flesh with the crème fraîche and half the lemon juice until smooth. Season well, and pour the remaining lemon juice on top. Chill until ready to serve.

Bring a large pot of water to a boil. Add the crabs and cook for 6 minutes, then plunge them into cold water. Remove their flesh and mix with the crème fraîche, lemon juice, and herbs. Season and chill. Mix most of the vinaigrette with the vegetables, and marinate for 10 minutes.

To serve, place a pastry cutter on each plate and spoon in the vegetables and crabmeat. Stir the lemon juice into the avocado cream, then spoon it onto each salad. Carefully remove the rings. Garnish with tomato, grapefruit segments, and mint leaves, and drizzle with the remaining vinaigrette around the bottom of the salad.

you will need

4 uncooked blue crabs

3 tbsp. crème fraîche, or heavy cream

2 tbsp. lemon juice

2 tsp. finely chopped mint

1 tsp. finely chopped tarragon

Salt and freshly ground black pepper

Lemon grass Vinaigrette (see page 154)

2 carrots, finely sliced

2 turnips, finely diced

Tomato quarters, pink grapefruit segments, and mint leaves, for garnishing

AVOCADO CREAM

2 large avocados

2 tbsp. crème fraîche, or heavy cream

Juice of 2 lemons

Serves 6

ravioli of goat cheese

In a bowl mix the goat cheese, cream cheese, and the herbs. Mold the mixture into little balls and place in the fridge.

Roll out the pasta dough using a pasta machine or rolling pin. Divide the sheet into 2 rectangles and keep one sheet covered with clean kitchen towel or plastic wrap, while you work with the other. Using 4-inch and 5-inch pastry cutters, cut out 2 discs of each size. Place one ball of filling in the center of each smaller disc, brush the edges with beaten egg, and top with a larger disc. Press the edges to seal. Repeat with the other rectangle. Blanch the ravioli for 1 minute in hot salted water and rinse under cold water. Coat with olive oil and cover with plastic wrap until ready to serve.

you will need

1lb. goat cheese

½ cup cream cheese

20 cilantro leaves, chopped

20 flat-leaf parsley leaves, chopped

20 chives, chopped

1 recipe Pasta Dough (see page 157)

1 egg, beaten

Olive oil

Serves 4

steamed cod on a warm salad
with champagne vinaigrette

you will need

⅔ cup olive oil

¼ cup Champagne Vinaigrette (see page 154)

2 red onions, diced

1 cucumber, cut into ½-inch dice

1lb. new potatoes, boiled

Salt and freshly ground black pepper

4 x 5oz. cod fillets

Serves 4

To make the potato salad, heat the olive oil and 3 tablespoons of the vinaigrette in a pan over a low heat. Add the red onion and cucumber, and heat gently for 2 minutes. Add the new potatoes, season with salt and pepper, and transfer to a dish to keep warm. Rinse out the pan.

Half-fill the pan with boiling water. Place the cod fillets in a steamer over the pan and steam for 4 minutes. Arrange some potato salad on each plate, and place a cod fillet on top. Drizzle with the remaining champagne vinaigrette.

I first tasted cappuccino soup eleven years ago, in a 3-star restaurant in France. The soup has been on the menu at Peacock Alley for five years now, and has become one of its trademarks. You do need a frying pan as well.

cappuccino of navy beans

with morels and seared scallops

you will need

1 cup dried navy beans, soaked overnight

Salt

1 small onion, peeled

1 carrot, peeled

1 sprig thyme

1 sprig rosemary

3½ cups Chicken or Vegetable Stock

(see page 153)

2 tbsp. butter

¼lb. morels

1–2 tsp. truffle oil

⅔ cup heavy cream

½ stick (¼ cup) butter, diced and chilled

1 tbsp. olive oil

4 scallops

Tarragon leaves, for garnishing

Sliced chiles, for garnishing

Bread sticks, for serving

Serves 4

Drain the beans, transfer to a large pot, and add enough lightly salted cold water to cover by 2 inches. Add the onion, carrot, and herbs. Bring to a boil, boil for 10 minutes, then lower the heat to a simmer. Cook for 25–30 minutes until soft. Drain and discard the onion, carrot and herbs. In a food processor, blend the beans to a fine purée. Rinse out the pot.

Pour the stock in the pot and cook for 5 minutes over a high heat until reduced slightly. Meanwhile, melt the butter in a frying pan and sauté the mushrooms for 2–3 minutes. Sprinkle with a little of the truffle oil. Transfer to a bowl, and wipe out the pot with paper towels.

Using a hand-held blender, mix the bean purée into the reduced stock until smooth, then whisk in the cream and remaining truffle oil. Divide the mushrooms among 4 cups. Reheat the soup and add the cold butter. Whisk with the hand-held blender until the mixture bubbles.

Heat the olive oil in the frying pan and sauté the scallops for 1 minute on each side. Pour the soup into the cups and place a skewered scallop on the side of each cup. Garnish with tarragon leaves and sliced chiles, and serve with bread sticks.

This may be a bit of a cholesterol special, but if you don't care, please eat it!

spaghetti carbonara

with peas and poached eggs

you will need

1 tbsp. malt vinegar

8 eggs

3 tbsp. olive oil

1lb. dried spaghetti

1¾ cups peas

¼lb. thick-sliced bacon, cut into
½-inch pieces

Salt and freshly ground black pepper

2 tbsp. crème fraîche or, if unavailable,
a mixture of heavy and sour cream

2 tbsp. finely chopped parsley

1½ cups freshly grated Parmesan

Serves 4

Quarter-fill a pot with boiling water and bring to a gentle simmer over medium heat. Add the vinegar, stirring the water to make a whirlpool, and crack 2 eggs into the center of the pot, and let them cook for 1–2 minutes. Remove from the pot with a slotted spoon and drain on paper towels. Repeat with another 2 eggs. Transfer the eggs to a bowl of cold water.

Fill the pot with salted water and bring to a boil. Add 1 tablespoon of olive oil and cook the spaghetti until al dente. Drain well and rinse with plenty of cold water. Drain again, drizzle with more olive oil, then transfer to a bowl.

Fill the pot with salted water, bring to a boil, and.add the peas. Cook for 3–4 minutes, and refresh under cold water, then drain well. Rinse out the pot.

Heat the remaining olive oil in the pot and cook the bacon over medium heat for 5–6 minutes until crispy. Add black pepper and cook for 1 minute. Add the spaghetti and peas, and toss until warmed through. Mix together the remaining eggs, crème fraîche, and parsley, and add to the pot. Remove from heat and stir constantly for 1 minute to allow the heat to cook the eggs.

To serve, stir in half the Parmesan and place the poached eggs on top of the spaghetti. Sprinkle with the remaining Parmesan to garnish.

shallow pan

The shallow pan is very versatile, suitable for many recipes. It allows you to prepare dishes such as ratatouille quickly. as all the vegetables are evenly spread over the heat source. I can not stress enough that the better the quality of your pan, the better the results. The ideal shallow pan has a large, round base of copper or steel. You can fry, stew, or poach with this pan.

For those who are bored with the more traditional ways of serving asparagus, this gives it a new twist without involving too much work.

provençal asparagus

you will need

2 tbsp. butter

1 shallot, finely diced

2 cloves garlic, crushed

1 sprig thyme

1 sprig rosemary

¼ cup Chicken Stock (see page 153)

Salt and freshly ground black pepper

24 asparagus spears, peeled and blanched for 1 minute

Small bunch of chives, finely chopped

Serves 4

Melt the butter in a large shallow pan over medium heat Add the shallot, garlic, and herbs, cover and sweat gently for 3–4 minutes without allowing it to color. Add the chicken stock, season well, and reduce heat to a gentle simmer. Add the asparagus for about 30 seconds, until heated through. Add the chopped chives just before serving.

This is an unusual recipe in that the ratatouille is quite dry, not like the usual stew of vegetables. Serve it with couscous or rice dishes.

ratatouille

with arugula and parmesan

you will need

2 tbsp. olive oil

2 shallots, chopped

4 cloves garlic, crushed

2 red bell peppers, seeded and finely diced

1 yellow bell pepper, seeded and finely diced

4 zucchini, finely diced

2 eggplants, finely diced

½ cup tomato paste

2 tsp. sugar

Salt and freshly ground black pepper

2 tbsp. white wine

1 tbsp. finely chopped basil

½lb. arugula

¼ cup Balsamic Vinaigrette (see page 154)

½ cup shaved Parmesan

Serves 4

Heat the oil in a pan. Add the shallots and garlic, and cover and sweat over gentle heat until soft.

Add all the vegetables and cook quickly over high heat. Add the tomato paste and cook for 1–2 minutes, stirring frequently. Season with sugar, salt, and pepper. Deglaze with white wine and add the basil.

Toss the arugula with the vinaigrette. To serve, spoon the ratatouille into a ring, dress with the salad, season, and garnish with Parmesan shavings.

Five years ago any monkfish caught in Irish waters would have been thrown back, or used as bait. Now it is very expensive, and will be almost extinct in another five years. If you can't find any choy sum to accompany, use bok choy or spinach.

medallion of monkfish

with soy sauce and choy sum

Blanch the choy sum in a pot of boiling, salted water for 3 minutes. Refresh under cold water, and drain well. Rinse out the pot.

Combine the lemon juice, garlic, grated ginger, and soy sauce in a bowl.

Place the oil in the pot over high heat and cook the monkfish for 1 minute on each side. Add the choy sum, carrot, scallions, and the garlic mixture. Increase heat and add the butter. Swirl the pan to incorporate the butter, season well, and sprinkle with the chile strips. Serve iimmediately.

you will need

2lbs. choy sum, shredded

Salt and freshly ground black pepper

Juice of 1 lemon

5 cloves garlic, crushed

1-inch ginger root, peeled and grated

2 tbsp. sweet soy sauce

1 tbsp. olive oil

2lbs. monkfish (also called angel fish) fillets, cut into 12 medallions

1 carrot, cut into thin strips

4 scallions, cut into thin strips

½ stick (¼ cup) butter, cubed

1 large red chile pepper, seeded and cut into strips

Serves 4

This is the perfect way of eating chocolate. The dish is rich but light, with none of that heavy chocolatey feeling.

hazelnut praline

you will need

⅔ cup light cream

¼lb. (about 1⅓ cups) white chocolate

¼lb. hazelnut nougat
(available in specialist shops)

2 tsp. pâté noisette
(available in specialist shops)

1 gelatin leaf, soaked in a small
amount of water

1 cup whipping cream,
lightly whipped

Ice-cream and chocolate curls,
for serving

Finely chopped hazelnuts,
for decoration

Serves 4

Put the cream in a pan and bring to a boil. Boil for 1–2 minutes, then add the white chocolate. When it starts to melt, mix in the nougat and pâté noisette. Remove from heat and let cool slightly, then add the gelatin as the mixture starts to cool down.

Fold in the whipped cream. Pour into dariole molds and freeze until set. To remove from the molds, dip the base in boiling water for 10 seconds and then invert on to a plate. Serve with vanilla, chocolate or white chocolate ice-cream, and chocolate curls. Sprinkle with finely chopped hazelnuts.

The perfect light dessert to end a heavy, rich meal – and it looks so beautiful.

poached pears in vanilla

with fromage blanc sorbet

Place all the syrup ingredients in a pot over low heat until the sugar is dissolved. When all the sugar has dissolved completely, boil for 30 minutes. Let it cool to 165°F.

Add the pears and cook for 30 minutes on low heat until the syrup has reduced to half. Transfer the pears to a shallow dish and strain the syrup over them. Wash out the pot.

For the sorbet, place the water, glucose, trimouline, and lemon juice in the pot and bring to a boil. Let the mixture cool and then add the fromage blanc. Process in an ice-cream machine for about 40 minutes, or freeze in a plastic container.

To serve, arrange each pear in the center of a large plate and decorate with a mint sprig. Pour some syrup around the pear and serve with a scoop of sorbet.

you will need

4 large, firm pears, peeled and cored,
   but left whole

Mint sprigs, for decoration

SYRUP

2 cups sugar

1 quart water

3 vanilla beans

Peel of 1 orange

Peel of 1 lemon

1 tsp. rose water

1 star anise

1 clove

FROMAGE BLANC SORBET

2 cups water

⅓ cup corn syrup

2 tbsp. trimouline (a water/sugar mixture)

¼ cup lemon juice

1lb. fromage blanc or, if unavailable, 2 cups
   cream cheese

Serves 4

The humble stewed apple is transformed when it is cooked with spices and served with vanilla-flavored crème fraîche

stewed apple with cinnamon,

five spice, crème fraîche, and vanilla

Place the lemon juice in a bowl, add the chopped apples, and roll them in the lemon juice to avoid discoloration.

you will need

Juice of 1 lemon

7 Golden Delicious or Granny Smith apples, peeled, cored, and chopped

3 tbsp. sweet butter

1 cinnamon stick

1 tbsp. five-spice powder

6 tbsp. sugar

6 tbsp. ground almonds

4 generous tbsp. crème fraîche or, if unavailable, heavy cream

1 vanilla bean

Serves 4

Heat a pan over medium heat and add the butter. Add the apple, cinnamon, and five-spice powder, and cook for 8 minutes. Add the sugar, and sprinkle with the ground almonds. Cook for a further 20 minutes over medium heat.

Mix the crème fraîche with the seeds from the vanilla bean. Serve the apples with a spoonful of crème fraîche.

frying pan

Frying pans have come in for a lot of bad press in recent years – own one, and your cholesterol level is obviously not a concern. But the recipes in this chapter do not involve large quantities of oil and fat. Non-stick frying pans with thick cast-iron or copper bases allow you to fry with little fat, since the heat is evenly spread over the pan.

Scallops are my favorite ingredient, hence there are a lot of scallop dishes in this book. In my spare time I go diving, hand-picking scallops off the coast of Cork and Donegal – they taste much better than the dredged ones.

seared scallops
with guacamole, cilantro, and chiles

you will need

1 avocado

Juice of 1 lemon

Juice of 1 lime

Salt and freshly ground black pepper

1 cup chopped cilantro

1 clove garlic, chopped

1 chile, seeded and diced

1 cup chopped chives

1 tbsp. olive oil

2 tbsp. butter

12 fresh scallops

2 tbsp. coconut milk

Cilantro sprigs, for garnishing

AVOCADO SALAD

1 avocado, diced

1 chile, seeded and diced

½ cup chopped cilantro

Serves 4

Peel and pit the avocado and dice it finely. Place in a small bowl, add the lemon and lime juice, and season with salt and pepper. Blend the cilantro, garlic, chile and chives in a food processor, then mix in with the avocado.

Heat the olive oil and butter in a small frying pan. Season the scallops, then sear for 1 minute on each side. Mix the ingredients for the salad in a bowl. Serve the scallops with spoonfuls of guacamole and avocado salad.

Garnish with coconut milk and coriander.

Creamy, fresh-tasting pea purée and crispy pancetta look wonderfully colorful and add a new dimension to the deep-sea flavor of the scallops

seared scallops

with crispy pancetta and pea purée

Heat half the butter in a large frying pan over gentle heat, add the shallots, cover, and sweat until just starting to soften. Add the peas and cook for 1 minute before adding the sugar, seasoning, and cream. Bring to a boil, then cook gently for about 15 minutes until the cream has reduced.

you will need

1 stick (½ cup) butter

2 shallots, roughly chopped

2 cups fresh or frozen peas

1 tsp. sugar

Salt and freshly ground black pepper

⅔ cup heavy cream

Juice of 1 lemon

12–20 scallops, depending on
   whether this is an appetizer or
   main course

8 thin slices pancetta

Salad leaves, for serving

Flat-leaf parsley, for garnishing

Purée the mixture in a food processor and if the mixture is not thick enough, return it to the frying pan and cook gently until it has thickened slightly. Season with the lemon juice and transfer to a serving dish. Keep warm.

Rinse out the pan and heat the remaining butter on high heat. Season the scallops well and sear on both sides for about 30–40 seconds. Add the pancetta and cook for another 1–2 minutes until the pancetta is crispy.

To serve, arrange the scallops on each plate with a slice of pancetta. Top with some salad leaves and another slice of pancetta, and finish with a spoonful of pea purée. Garnish with sprigs of flat-leaf parsley.

My favorite ingredient again! Quick, easy, and delicious, these seared scallops make the ideal appetizer. Try to get fresh ones – the frozen variety tend to be very watery.

seared scallops

with arugula and parmesan salad

Heat the oil in a frying pan. Season the scallops and fry for 1 minute on each side until golden. Turn off the heat and keep the scallops warm.

Mix the arugula with the Parmesan shavings in a salad bowl. Add the vinaigrette, the scallops, and their juices. Toss the salad to coat everything well in the vinaigrette, and serve immediately.

you will need

2 tbsp. peanut oil

Salt and freshly ground black pepper

12 scallops

4 handfuls arugula leaves

2 cups shaved or grated Parmesan

1 recipe quantity Balsamic

Vinaigrette (see page 154)

Serves 4

capellini cakes

you will need

7oz. capellini or angel hair pasta, soaked in
boiling water until al dente

⅓ cup olive oil

½ stick (¼ cup) butter

2 tbsp. finely grated Parmesan

Salt and freshly ground black pepper

Serves 4

Drain the pasta and toss in a large bowl with 4 tablespoons of the olive oil, the butter, and Parmesan. Season well. Arrange the pasta in 4 x 3½-inch metal rings. Heat the remaining olive oil in a large frying pan. Using a spatula, transfer the rings to the pan and sauté the pasta gently for 1–2 minutes on both sides.

Finish by broiling the pasta cakes under low heat for 2–3 minutes until crispy. Serve the cakes immediately, with broiled or barbecued meat or chicken.

pan-fried squid
with chile

Slit the squid down one side and lay them out flat. Make small criss-cross cuts in the squid, using a sharp knife. Mix half the olive oil, garlic, chile, and lemon juice in a bowl and add the squid. Toss to coat, and leave to marinate for 15 minutes.

Heat a large frying pan until smoking, then add the remaining oil. Drain the squid, reserving the marinade, and put in the pan. Season with salt and pepper. Toss the squid in the pan for about 3 minutes, then add the reserved marinade and the chopped parsley. Mix well and serve immediately.

you will need

2lbs. baby squid

3 tbsp. olive oil

1 clove garlic, crushed

1 red chile, seeded and finely chopped

Juice of 1 lemon

Salt and freshly ground black pepper

Handful of flat-leaf parsley, chopped

Serves 4

I hadn't cooked omelettes in years, until my daughter went through an omelette phase while we were trying to get some protein into her. This is her favorite.

crab omelette

with braised scallions and cilantro

Melt one-third of the butter in a frying pan and sauté the scallions for a few minutes. Season and add the sugar. Add a few tablespoons of water if they start to burn, and let the water evaporate. When they are just wilted, remove from the pan and keep warm. Wipe the pan clean with paper towels.

Mix the cream and crabmeat together and season well. Pour the olive oil in the pan over medium heat, and add the remaining butter. Whisk the eggs and season well. Dice the remaining butter and add to the egg mixture.

Pour the eggs into the frying pan and swirl around, drawing the outside to the center with a wooden spatula, and letting the liquid set. Turn the heat low, and spoon the crab mixture and half the cilantro into the center. Fold over the sides of the omelette and gently slide onto a plate. Sprinkle with chopped cilantro, and serve with the warm scallions and a green salad.

you will need

2½ sticks (1¼ cups) butter

16 scallions, trimmed

Salt and freshly ground black pepper

2 tsp. sugar

½ cup heavy cream

10oz. fresh crabmeat

3 tbsp. olive oil

12 eggs

3 tbsp. chopped cilantro

Green salad, for serving

Serves 4

This recipe cheats slightly by using two pans – you will need a pot to cook the tagliatelle and heat the sauce – but I hope you agree the end result is worth the extra washing up.

roasted monkfish

with tagliatelle and cream

you will need

1lb. tagliatelle

Salt and freshly ground black pepper

½ cup olive oil

4 x 6oz. fillets of monkfish

2 cups heavy cream

1 clove garlic, crushed

¼ cup chopped fresh sage

Serves 4

Preheat the oven to 400°F.

Boil the tagliatelle in a large pot of boiling, salted water until al dente. Drain, rinse under cold water, and drain again. Toss the tagliatelle in half the olive oil, and set aside. Rinse out the pot.

Heat the remaining olive oil in a large ovenproof frying pan. Season the monkfish with plenty of salt and pepper, and sear on all sides for 2–3 minutes. Transfer to the oven to finish cooking for 7 minutes.

Place the cream, garlic and sage in the large pot and bring to a boil. Season well and cook until reduced slightly. Add the tagliatelle and toss well. Serve with the monkfish.

Wild salmon are in season in Ireland from June to August. During these months I go fishing every Sunday, from Blessington in County Wicklow to Lough Foyle.

roasted salmon

with saffron cream sauce

you will need

4 x 6oz. salmon fillets,
   skinned and boned

2 tbsp. vegetable oil

Salt and freshly ground white pepper

1lb. spinach, precooked in a little
   butter, drained and kept warm

1 pat of butter

12 Gnocchi (see page 33)

SAFFRON CREAM SAUCE

½ stick (¾ cup) sweet butter,
   chilled and diced

2 shallots, chopped

1 clove garlic, crushed

1 cup dry white wine

½ cup whipping cream

Pinch of saffron

Serves 4

First make the sauce. Melt half the butter in a deep heavy frying pan and add the shallots and garlic. Cover and sweat over medium heat until soft. Add the white wine and boil until the sauce has reduced to ¼ cup. Pour in the cream, add the saffron, and boil again for 1 minute. Start to whisk in the remaining butter, a cube at a time, and continue to whisk until the butter is well incorporated. Season with salt and pepper, and remove from heat. Pour the sauce into a bowl and keep warm. Wash out the pan.

Cut the salmon fillets into 4 even slices and season with salt and pepper. Heat the vegetable oil in the frying pan over medium heat. Place the salmon in the pan and cook for 4 minutes, then turn and cook for 3 minutes on the other side. This will cook the salmon to a golden brown. Meanwhile, reheat the spinach in a small pan with a pat of butter, season, and drain.

To serve, spoon the sauce on to each plate. Arrange 3 gnocchi on the plate, and place the salmon slices in the center with the spinach carefully placed on top.

Another elegant stuffed omelette, this time with a Thai flavor, using garlic, cilantro, and fish sauce, to give an intriguing piquancy to the stuffing.

omelette stuffed

with ground pork

Heat a large frying pan and add 2 tablespoons of the oil. Add the garlic, and sweat over gentle heat until golden, then add the onion. Cook for 1 minute, then add the pork and stir-fry for 6–8 minutes. Stir in the fish sauce, then add the tomatoes and sugar. Simmer until the sauce begins to thicken, then remove from heat and stir in the chopped cilantro. Season the mixture and transfer to a bowl. Wipe the pan clean with paper towels.

Beat the eggs in a bowl with the water. Heat the frying pan over medium heat and add the remaining oil. Pour in the eggs and roll around until the surface of the pan is covered. Cook until the egg is almost cooked through, then remove from the heat. Spoon the pork mixture across the center of the egg and fold either side over the filling. Tip the omelette onto a large plate and sprinkle with cilantro leaves.

you will need

5 tbsp. vegetable oil

4 cloves garlic, crushed

1 small onion, finely chopped

¼ lb. ground pork

2 tsp. naam pla fish sauce
    (available from Asian markets)

10 cherry tomatoes, quartered

2 tsp. sugar

2 tbsp. chopped cilantro

Salt and freshly ground black
    pepper

6 eggs

1 tsp. water

Cilantro leaves, for garnishing

Serves 4

The rich sweetness of the beet confit goes well with the slightly gamey flavor of guinea fowl, now widely available.

roasted guinea fowl
with confit of beets

Preheat the oven to 400°F.

you will need

½ cup olive oil

1 free-range guinea fowl, cut into 6 joints

4 cooked beets, peeled and cubed

2 tbsp. red wine vinegar

5 sprigs thyme

1 cup water

Salt and freshly ground black pepper

Serves 4

Heat half the oil in a large ovenproof frying pan and sear the guinea fowl joints for 4 minutes on each side. Add the beets, vinegar, thyme, and water. Season well. Transfer the pan to the preheated oven and roast for 30 minutes.

Remove the guinea fowl pieces with a slotted spoon and place on a large serving dish, letting the juices drain into the beets. Place the pan on top of the stove over high heat, to let the water evaporate. Add the remaining olive oil, season well, and serve with the guinea fowl.

Fillet of beef is the best cut of meat that you can buy, renowned for its exquisite tenderness. It is often served with equally luxurious accompaniments, but braised Belgian endive gives a lighter, more modern touch.

peppered beef fillet

with braised Belgian endive

Mix the marinade ingredients in a shallow dish. Add the beef, turn to coat it, and let it marinate for 2–3 hours.

Heat the olive oil in a large frying pan over high heat. Add the endive, flat sides down, and char for a few minutes. Add the butter and sprinkle on the sugar. Season well and when the mixture starts to caramelize, turn down the heat. Add a few tablespoons of water, and turn the endive so they cook on both sides. Turn up the heat, and when they are golden and starting to caramelize, transfer to a warm plate.

Wipe the pan clean with paper towels. Drain the beef and heat 2 tablespoons of the marinade in the pan. Add the beef and sear on both sides over very high heat, about 3–4 minutes for medium rare.

Allow to rest for a minute, then serve with the endive and drizzle with aïoli.

you will need

4 beef fillet steaks, about 7oz. each

¼ cup olive oil

4 heads Belgian endive, sliced in half
   lengthwise

1 stick (½ cup) butter

3 tsp. sugar

Salt and freshly ground black pepper

Aïoli, for serving

MARINADE

½ cup olive oil

2 tbsp. coarse ground black pepper

2 tsp. coarse salt

2 tsp. Worcestershire sauce

Serves 4

I have been a big fan of maple syrup ever since I lived in the States. It has the same effect as honey, but with a much more distinctive flavor.

maple-glazed pears

with spiced cream

Whip the cream with the cardamom and confectioners sugar, then refrigerate until ready to serve.

you will need

1¼ cups heavy cream

½ tsp. ground cardamom

1 tbsp. confectioners sugar

½ stick (¼ cup) butter

4 pears, cored, peeled, and sliced into quarters

4 tbsp. maple syrup

Serves 4

Melt the butter in a large frying pan over medium heat. Add the pears, and sauté for 2–3 minutes. Add the maple syrup, and gently turn the pears so that they become slightly caramelized on all sides.

Remove from heat and let cool. Serve with spoonfuls of the spiced cream.

sauté pan

If you only have one pan in your kitchen cupboard, make it a sauté pan. It should be made of lined copper, but stainless steel is more common. The wider the pan, the better, and it should have low sides to allow steam to escape. The lid is optional, but it does help in some recipes which need a lot of heat. If the handles are also steel, the sauté pan can be transferred to the oven to finish off the cooking.

This dish was first cooked in the restaurant by Steve Brewer, a close friend whose passion both for foie gras and cooking goes beyond anything.

brewer's foie gras

Season the foie gras and place in a sauté pan over high heat. Sear on both sides then remove from the heat and reserve. Rinse out the pan.

you will need

4 x ¼lb. slices of foie gras (goose liver pate)

Salt and freshly ground black pepper

2½ cups water

2 tbsp. orange-blossom water

¼ cup sugar

2 tbsp. lemon juice

2 tbsp. orange juice

1 vanilla bean

24 orange segments

2 tbsp. butter, cut up

Watercress, for serving or,

if unavailable, use arugula

Sliced chiles, for serving

Deep-fried salsify strips, for garnishing

(optional)

Serves 4

Make a syrup by combining the water, orange-blossom water, sugar, lemon juice, and orange juice in the pan. Add the vanilla bean and cook for 8–10 minutes. Strain the syrup through a sieve into a bowl, removing the vanilla bean. Split the bean, scrape out the seeds, and add them to the syrup. Rinse out the pan.

Return the foie gras to the pan and sauté over medium heat until golden brown. Add the orange segments. Pour in the syrup and cook until it has reduced to a thick sauce. When ready to serve, add the butter.

To serve, sprinkle with watercress and sliced chile. Garnish with strips of deep-fried salsify, if using.

A dramatic presentation using the aptly named trompettes de la mort lifts a simple pasta dish out of the ordinary.

penne

with trompettes de la mort

Fill a large sauté pan with water, add 2 tablespoons of the olive oil, and bring to a boil. Add the penne and cook for about 8 minutes, or until al dente. Drain, refresh in ice-cold water, and store in the fridge on a tray until ready to serve.

Heat 1 tablespoon of the oil in the sauté pan, add the trompettes, and sweat over gentle heat for 2–3 minutes. Remove from the pan and set aside.

Heat the remaining oil in the pan, add the shallots, garlic, and dried mushrooms, and sweat over gentle heat until the shallots and garlic are softened but not colored. Add the chicken stock, increase the heat, and simmer until reduced by half. Add the cream, and again simmer until reduced by half. Add the pasta to the sauce, season well, and heat through gently.

Serve the penne in the sauce, sprinkled with chopped chervil, and arrange some trompettes on each serving.

you will need

¼ cup olive oil

6oz. dried penne

¼ lb. fresh trompettes de la mort
(also known as black chanterelles)

4 shallots, finely sliced

2 cloves garlic, finely sliced

1oz. (about ⅔ to 1 cup) mixed
dried mushrooms, soaked in warm
water for 20 minutes and drained

2½ cups Chicken Stock
(see page 153)

⅔ cup heavy cream

Salt and freshly ground black
pepper

2 tbsp. chopped fresh chervil

Serves 4

Don't worry if you don't possess a sauté pan – these delicious Chinese-style shrimp could also be cooked in a frying pan or a wok.

pan-fried shrimp

with chiles, ginger, cilantro, and bok choy

Heat a large sauté pan and pour in the sesame oil. Add the garlic, chiles and ginger and sauté for about 30 seconds over a high heat.

you will need

2 tbsp. sesame oil

1 clove garlic, diced

1 red chile, seeded and diced

1 green chile, seeded and diced

1-inch ginger root, peeled and finely diced

2lbs. jumbo shrimp, shelled and deveined

2lbs. bok choy, leaves separated

1 tbsp. honey

2 tbsp. soy sauce

Juice of 1 lime

Salt and freshly ground black pepper

Cilantro leaves, for garnishiing

Serves 4

Place the prawns in the pan with the bok choy and sauté for 1 minute. Add the honey, soy sauce and lime juice. Simmer for 1 minute, season and serve sprinkled with coriander leaves.

My favorite ingredient again, this time teamed with caramelized apples and sauté potatoes to give a combination of flavors that is quite irresistible.

scallops

with caramelized apples and sauté potatoes

Heat the oil in a large sauté pan over medium heat. Add the potato slices and sauté until tender and golden brown. Remove the potatoes with a slotted spoon and keep warm.

Add the scallops to the hot pan and sauté for about 1 minute on one side and 30 seconds on the other side. Remove with a slotted spoon and keep warm.

Sprinkle the apples with the sugar and add to the pan over a high heat. Pour in the cider and white wine, and boil until reduced by half. Remove the apples with a slotted spoon and add the chicken stock. Return to a boil and reduce by half.

Return the potatoes, scallops, and apples to the pan, and cook for another minute. Season with salt and pepper and serve while hot.

you will need

4 large baking potatoes, cut into ¼-inch thick slices

3 tbsp. olive oil

8 large scallops, sliced in half

4 Granny Smith apples, peeled, cored, and chopped

3 tbsp. sugar

3 tbsp. cider

3 tbsp. white wine

½ cup Chicken Stock (see page 153)

Salt and freshly ground black pepper

Serves 4

Pasta ribbons and oyster mushrooms in a creamy mustard sauce are the perfect accompaniment for tender rabbit loin.

pappardelle with rabbit loin,

mustard and parsley

Cook the pappardelle in a large sauté pan of boiling salted water until al dente. Drain and set aside. Rinse out the pan.

you will need

4oz. dried pappardelle or other broad egg noodle

Salt and freshly ground black pepper

½ stick (¼ cup) butter

8 rabbit loins

2 shallots, diced

1 clove garlic, diced

10 oyster mushrooms

⅔ cup white wine

1¼ cup Chicken Stock (see page 153)

1 tbsp. wholegrain mustard

1 tbsp. heavy cream

1 tbsp. chopped flat-leaf parsley

10–12 blanched spinach leaves (optional)

Serves 4

Heat half the butter in the pan over medium heat. Season the rabbit and sauté for about 10 minutes on each side, or until cooked through, then remove from the pan and keep warm.

Add the remaining butter to the pan and sauté the shallots, garlic, and oyster mushrooms for 2 minutes. Add the white wine and bring to a boil, reducing the mixture by half, then add the stock and reduce again. Add the rabbit, mustard, and cream, and mix in the pappardelle. Let simmer for 3 minutes, until the pasta is heated through. Add the chopped parsley and season to taste.

For an optional presentation, as shown here, take half the cooked rabbit and cut into medallions. Wrap the rabbit pieces in blanched spinach leaves, return to the pan, and warm through.

Puy lentils, richly flavored with smoked bacon, garlic, and onions, are the perfect foil to tender slices of calf's liver. The final addition of balsamic vinegar enhances the rich taste.

calf's liver and bacon
with Puy lentils

Pour the oil into a large sauté pan over a medium-high heat. Season the liver and seal in the hot oil on both sides, then remove from the pan and keep warm.

Add the bacon, garlic, and onions to the pan and sauté until golden brown. Drain the lentils and add to the pan along with the chicken stock. Let simmer for 1½–2 hours.

Return the liver to the pan and cook with the lentils for another 10 minutes. Mix in the balsamic vinegar and serve sprinkled with chopped parsley.

you will need

¼ cup olive oil

Salt and freshly ground black pepper

¾lb. calf's liver, sliced

½lb. bacon, cut into strips

2 cloves garlic, crushed

20 pearl onions

4oz. Puy lentils (French lentils, also known as Verte du Puy), soaked for 24 hours

2½ cups Chicken Stock (see page 153)

¼ cup balsamic vinegar

¼ cup chopped parsley

Serves 4

Fresh cépes are among the best of all mushrooms, with a deep, rich flavor.
Sautéed with fresh herbs and cream, they taste divine.

sautéed cépes with wild arugula

thyme, rosemary, and cream

Cook the penne in a large sauté pan of boiling salted water for about 8 minutes, until al dente, then drain and transfer to a bowl. Rinse out the pan.

Melt the butter in the pan over medium heat and sauté the cépes, shallots, and garlic for 3 minutes. Add the pasta and mix thoroughly. Pour in the chicken stock and simmer for 1 minute. Add the rosemary and thyme, simmer for a further minute, and pour in the cream. Bring to a boil and season.

Add the arugula at the last minute. Toss well and serve.

you will need

1lb. dried penne

Salt and freshly ground black pepper

½ stick (¼ cup) butter

½lb. fresh cépes mushrooms (also known as
    porcini), trimmed

2 shallots, diced

1 clove garlic, diced

1 cup Chicken Stock (see page 153)

1 sprig rosemary, chopped

2 springs thyme, chopped

⅔ cup heavy cream

2 bunches arugula

Serves 4

casserole dish

For these recipes you need a casserole dish that is equally happy on top of the stove or in the oven, so the bottom should be thick and heavy enough to withstand the heat. The most popular makes are usually cast iron, sometimes lined with enamel, and should last a lifetime with careful use and maintenance.

The baby eggplants here are chargrilled for a more dramatic presentation, but they could be cooked in the casserole with the chicken, if you prefer.

thai green curry
with baby eggplants and sticky rice

you will need

1 chicken, cut into 6 joints

Salt and freshly ground black pepper

3 tbsp. olive oil

1 cup Chicken Stock (see page 153)

4 lime leaves

2-inch piece of fresh galangal

½ cup coconut milk

2 tbsp. Thai green curry paste

¾ cup coconut cream

2 tbsp. naam pla fish sauce

1 tbsp. chopped cilantro

Juice of ½ lime

LIME STOCK

2 stalks lemon grass

½-inch piece ginger root

1 clove garlic

½ chile, seeded

½ lime

BABY EGGPLANTS

8 baby eggplants, cut in half

¼ cup olive oil

1 tsp. coarse salt

Serves 4

Place all the lime stock ingredients in a casserole dish and simmer for 15 minutes. Bring to a boil and continue to boil until reduced by a quarter. Strain the stock and rinse the casserole.

Season the chicken pieces with salt and pepper. Heat the olive oil in a large casserole dish and brown the chicken over medium heat. Cover the pan, reduce the heat, and cook for 25 minutes, turning the chicken pieces occasionally.

Meanwhile, prepare the baby eggplants. Preheat a chargrill or griddle pan. Rub the eggplants with olive oil and course salt, and grill for about 5 minutes on each side, or until tender.

Combine the chicken stock, lime leaves, and galangal in a large pan. Bring to a boil, then remove from the heat and let it infuse for 15 minutes. Strain the stock and return to the pan. Add the lime stock and boil vigorously for about 15 minutes, or until reduced by half.

Stir in the coconut milk, curry paste, fish sauce, and coconut cream, then add the chicken pieces. Sprinkle with the chopped cilantro and lime juice. Serve with the baby eggplants and sticky rice.

The robust red wine sauce goes well with the firm flesh of the monkfish.

braised monkfish

with navy beans, pearl onions, and red wine sauce

Preheat the oven to 350°F.

Heat a large casserole dish over medium heat and add the olive oil and butter. Season the monkfish, add to the dish, and cook for about 1 minute on all sides to seal. Remove the fish with a slotted spoon and keep warm.

Add the pearl onions, garlic, and thyme, and brown for a few minutes. Pour in the red wine and chicken stock. Drain the navy beans and add to the casserole. Cover, and cook in the preheated oven for about 1 hour, or until the beans are tender.

Add the monkfish, cover, and return to the oven for a further 10 minutes. Season to taste and serve immediately.

you will need

2 tbsp. olive oil

½ stick (¼ cup) butter

Salt and freshly ground black pepper

2lbs. monkfish tails, trimmed

14oz. pearl onions

4 cloves garlic, crushed

4 large sprigs thyme

1 bottle of dark red wine

1 quart Chicken Stock
  (see page 153)

½lb. navy beans,
  soaked overnight

Serves 4

Remember to allow time to soak the lentils overnight, otherwise this dish with its subtle amalgam of flavors is quick and easy to prepare.

smoked chicken

with mixed salad and Puy lentils

Mix the olive oil, balsamic vinegar, and shallots in a bowl and leave for 2 hours.

Combine the lentils, chicken stock, carrot, onion, and garlic in a casserole dish and simmer for 40 minutes. Drain and cool.

you will need

⅔ cup olive oil

6 tbsp. balsamic vinegar

2 shallots, finely diced

4 oz. Puy lentils (French lentils, also known as Verte du Puy), soaked overnight and drained

1 quart Chicken Stock (see page 153)

1 carrot, chopped

½ onion, chopped

½ head of garlic, peeled and crushed

4 breasts of smoked chicken, finely chopped

8 oz. mixed greens, such as arugula, lettuce, oak leaf, and mizuma

Serves 4

Mix half the shallot vinaigrette with the lentils, and let sit for 30 minutes. Mix the chicken into the lentils. Toss the salad leaves with the remaining vinaigrette and serve with the chicken and lentils.

Paprika, with its mild flavor and striking color, is an important ingredient in Hungarian cooking, and especially in this traditional meat stew. Make sure your paprika is fresh, and do not be tempted to use chile powder as a substitute – it is much too hot.

hungarian beef goulash

Preheat the oven to 400°F. Heat the butter in a large, heavy casserole dish, season the rump, and add to the dish. Add the onions and cook for 2 minutes, stirring. Add the paprika and flour, mix well, and place in the preheated oven, uncovered, for 10 minutes.

you will need

1 stick (½ cup) butter

2lbs. rump, cut into cubes

Salt and freshly ground black pepper

1lb. onions, chopped

¼ cup paprika

½ cup flour

1 tbsp. tomato paste

2 quarts Beef Stock (see page 153)

½lb. carrots, cut into chunks

1lb. potatoes, peeled and cut into chunks

Chopped parsley, for garnishing

Serves 4

Remove from the oven and mix in the tomato paste. Reduce the oven temperature to 350°. Add enough of the stock to cover the meat. Bring to a boil on top of the stove, and season. Cover with a lid and return to the oven for 2 hours.

After 1½ hours, mix in the chopped carrots and potatoes, and cook for another 30 minutes, or until the meat and vegetables are tender. Sprinkle with chopped parsley to serve.

braised ham hocks

with thyme and rosemary

Rinse the ham hocks and place in a large, heavy casserole dish with the carrots, onion, celery, garlic, thyme, and water. Bring to a boil on top of the stove, then reduce the heat to very low and simmer for 4 hours.

Strain, reserving the cooking liquid, and discard the vegetables and flavorings. Return the liquid to the casserole dish, and over high heat reduce to about 2¼ cups. Preheat the oven to 300°F.

Return the hocks to the casserole dish, along with the braising vegetables, and turn to coat with the reduced liquid. Transfer the casserole dish to the preheated oven and glaze for 45 minutes. Sprinkle the hocks with chopped parsley and serve with mashed potatoes.

you will need

4 ham hocks (shank portions), soaked for 12 hours in cold water

2 carrots, sliced

1 onion, sliced

2 stalks celery, chopped

½ head garlic

2 sprigs thyme

5 quarts water

BRAISING VEGETABLES

4 medium carrots

2 small turnips

6 cloves garlic

Chopped parsley, for serving

Serves 4

A new look for an old favorite. Peas and fava beans can be added at the last minute to give a touch of green and a summery feel to this dish.

modern irish stew

with thyme and rosemary

Place the lamb in a heavy casserole dish, along with the water and salt, and bring to a boil. Skim any fat off the surface and simmer for 30 minutes. Add half the potatoes and simmer for another 30 minutes, stirring to break up the potatoes.

Add the remaining potatoes, the other vegetables, and the thyme and rosemary. Simmer for 30 minutes or until the vegetables and meat are tender.

Stir in the parsley, cream, and butter, and serve. If using peas and beans, stir them in at the last minute.

you will need

2lbs. boneless shoulder, neck, or shank of lamb,
   trimmed of fat and cut into cubes

1 quart water

Salt

½lb. potatoes, peeled and cut into coarse chunks

½lb. carrots, thickly sliced (about 1½ cups)

½lb. leeks, thickly sliced (about 2⅓ cups)

½lb. pearl onions

2 sprigs thyme

2 sprigs rosemary

8oz. parsley, chopped (about 4 cups)

1 cup heavy cream

1 tbsp. sweet butter

2 cups fresh peas, cooked (optional)

½lb. fresh fava beans, cooked (optional)

Serves 4

roasting pan

This is a rectangular, metal, low-sided pan. The sides should be low to allow direct heat to come into contact with a joint of meat, but high enough to contain the juices from the food. The juices can often be used to make a thicker sauce or gravy, so the roasting pan should be heavy enough to withstand the heat of the stove top.

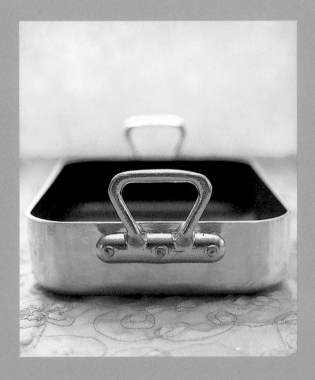

This is one of those dishes that more or less cooks itself while you get on with something else. The end result is really tasty, perfect for a cold winter's night.

braised lamb shanks

with thyme, roast carrot, and pearl onions

you will need

2 tbsp. olive oil

4 lamb shanks, trimmed of excess fat and knuckle removed

½lb. (about 1½ cups) carrots, cut into chunks

12 pearl onions

3 sprigs thyme

2 tbsp. water

Salt and freshly ground black pepper

2 tbsp. butter

1 tbsp. chopped flat-leaf parsley

1 tbsp. chopped thyme

Serves 4

Preheat the oven to 300°F.

Heat the oil in a large roasting pan on the stove. Brown the shanks on all sides, then remove from the pan. Add the carrots and onions, and cook until golden brown, then remove from the pan.

Return the lamb shanks and any juices to the roasting pan. along with the thyme sprigs and water. Season with salt and pepper, then place in the oven and cook for 2 hours, turning occasionally. Return the carrots and onions to the pan and continue to cook for 1 hour.

Remove from the oven and transfer the lamb shanks and vegetables to warm plates. Remove the thyme sprigs. Skim off the fat from the juices in the roasting pan, then bring to a boil on the stove. Reduce for a few minutes until it has the consistency of a light sauce. Remove from heat, add the butter, and season to taste.

Spoon some sauce over each shank and garnish with the chopped parsley and thyme.

Squab (baby pigeon) is much more tender than the adult wild pigeon and has a milder flavor. It is also much more expensive. If you can't find it, substitute with Cornish hen. Allow one per person.

roast squab

with green olives, saffron, and preserved lemon

you will need

2 tsp. hot paprika

2 tsp. turmeric

2 tsp. ground cumin

½ cup plus 1 tbsp.olive oil

6 x 3oz. squabs

24 red shallots

2 tbsp. ghee or clarified butter

6 cloves garlic, crushed

2 tsp. freshly minced ginger root

¼lb. squab livers

5 cups squab stock or Chicken Stock (see page 153)

12 large green olives, pitted and quartered

1 tsp. saffron

1 preserved lemon, finely chopped

2 tbsp. lemon juice

½ tsp. freshly ground black pepper

3 tbsp. sweet butter, diced

1 tbsp. chopped cilantro leaves.

Serves 6

Preheat the oven to 400°F. Mix half the paprika, turmeric, and cumin with the olive oil. Brush the squabs inside and out with the spiced olive oil.

Slice half the shallots. Heat the ghee in a large, heavy roasting pan over medium heat. Add the sliced shallots, garlic, ginger, and squab livers, and fry for 2 minutes. Add the remaining paprika, turmeric, and cumin, and cook for another 2 minutes. Pour in the stock and bring to a boil, then reduce the heat and simmer until the stock has reduced by half.

Strain the sauce through a fine sieve, return to the pan, and bring to a boil. Add the remaining shallots and simmer for 15 minutes. Add the olives, saffron, and preserved lemon, and simmer for another 5 minutes, then remove from heat. Pour the sauce into a bowl and keep warm.

With the roasting pan over high heat, add the tablespoon of oil. Add the squabs and cook for 2–3 minutes, turning until seared on all sides. Transfer to the preheated oven, and roast for 8 minutes. Remove the squabs from the pan and keep warm.

Return the sauce to the pan to warm it through. Whisk in the lemon juice, pepper, and butter, and stir in the cilantro. Place a squab in the center of each plate and pour the sauce around the edge. Serve whole or cut in half.

In Donegal there used to be a famous saying: the potatoes were so good, they ate the skins and all. Years ago, people would have had a heart attack if asked to peel the potatoes before cooking – peeling was done after cooking, if at all.

roast new potatoes

with coarse salt and rosemary

Preheat the oven to 350°F. Place the potatoes in a large roasting pan, drizzle with the olive oil, and sprinkle with 2 teaspoons of the salt and with the pepper. Bake in the preheated oven for about 30 minutes, or until the potatoes are golden brown and starting to shrivel slightly.

you will need

1½ lbs. baby new potatoes

½ cup olive oil

3 tsp. coarse salt

Freshly ground black pepper

5 sprigs rosemary

2 cloves garlic, crushed

½ stick (¼ cup) butter

Serves 4

Add the rosemary, garlic, and butter. Shake the roasting pan and bake for another 10 minutes. These potatoes may be served hot or warm, sprinkled with the remaining salt.

These confit potatoes could not be simpler to cook, but the taste is out of this world. They are perfect to serve with duck or squab, and are also very good cooked over a barbecue.

confit sweet potatoes
with garlic and thyme

Preheat the oven to 350°F.

you will need

1lb. sweet potatoes, cut into
¼-inch thick slices

1 cup olive oil

Coarse salt

Freshly ground black pepper

2 cloves garlic, crushed

2 sprigs thyme

¼ cup balsamic vinegar

Serves 4

Place the potatoes in a roasting pan, drizzle with half the olive oil, and sprinkle very generously with coarse salt and black pepper. Bake for 30 minutes, or until tender, shaking the pan occasionally to prevent them sticking.

Five minutes before they are ready, add the garlic and thyme. Shake the potatoes well and cook for another few minutes. Drizzle with the remaining olive oil and the balsamic vinegar. Serve immediately.

chargrill & grill

Chargrilling covers the use of several utensils – griddle pans, grill pans, and even barbecues. The beauty of chargrilling is that the food is cooked quickly and without mess. When the food has been marinated or coated, little oil is needed since chargrilling at high temperatures cooks the food in its own juices. When the food is to be coated in olive oil, make sure it is only a light coating, and that you use a high-quality oil.

Squid is now very trendy, and can be found cooked in all sorts of ways. It makes perfect barbecue food, and has the great advantage that it is easy to cook and can stand up to strong flavors.

chile, salt, and pepper squid

with vermicelli

you will need

3 red chiles, seeded and finely chopped

1 tbsp. sea salt flakes or Kosher salt

1 tsp. freshly ground black pepper

12 baby squid, cut in half

2 tbsp. olive oil

4oz. rice vermicelli

2 tbsp. soy sauce

2 tbsp. lime juice

3 tbsp. cilantro leaves

1 tbsp. brown sugar

2 tbsp. naam pla fish sauce

Serves 4

Mix the chiles, salt, and pepper in a bowl. Brush the squid lightly with oil then dip the pieces into the bowl to coat with the chile mixture.

Place the rice vermicelli in a bowl and pour on enough boiling water to cover. Let soak for 5 minutes, or until tender, then drain. Toss the vermicelli with the soy sauce, lime juice, cilantro, sugar, and fish sauce. Divide the vermicelli between four serving bowls.

To cook the squid, preheat a chargrill or frying pan over medium heat. Add the squid and cook for 10–15 seconds on each side. Arrange the squid on top of the vermicelli and serve immediately.

Salmon is ideal for grilling or chargrilling, being an oily fish. It goes perfectly with Mediterranean vegetables, with a spoonful of pesto on top. This makes a very good lunch dish, since it is so easy to prepare.

chargrilled salmon

with mediterranean vegetables and pesto

Brush the vegetables and salmon with olive oil and season heavily. Place the potatoes and onions on the chargrill for about 15 minutes, turning occasionally to get a criss-cross effect. Repeat with the peppers, zucchini and eggplants.

Half way through cooking the vegetables, place the salmon on the grill, skin-side down, and cook for about 3 minutes on both sides.

Serve the salmon and vegetables with some pesto on each plate.

you will need

8 large new potatoes, boiled and skinned

2 red onions, quartered

2 red bell peppers, seeded and quartered

2 yellow bell peppers, seeded and quartered

2 zucchini, sliced lengthways

2 eggplants, sliced lengthwise

4 x 6oz. fillets of wild salmon

3 tbsp. olive oil

Salt and freshly ground black pepper

½ cup Basil Pesto (see page 155)

Serves 4

A simple dish, ideal for lunch. Remember to allow time to marinate the salmon overnight. Mesclun, a mixture of salad leaves, usually features among others bok choy and rocket.

ginger-glazed salmon

with mesclun and ginger

Mix all the ingredients for the marinade together in a shallow dish. Add the salmon, turn to coat well, and let it marinate in the fridge overnight.

you will need

4 x 6oz. salmon fillets

4 handfuls mesclun (gourmet salad mix)

¼ cup vinaigrette

MARINADE

¼ cup olive oil

2 tbsp. soft brown sugar

4-inch piece ginger root , peeled
  and grated

2 tbsp. sea salt or Kosher salt

freshly ground black pepper

Serves 4

Preheat the broiler to high. Line the broiler pan with foil and oil well. Lay the salmon on it and broil on both sides for 1 minute. The salmon will be a little rare in the middle. If you prefer it well done, simply broil for a few minutes longer .

Toss the salad leaves with the vinaigrette and arrange in the center of each plate. Place the salmon fillets on top and serve immediately.

Oven-dried tomatoes, so easy to prepare, have a rich sweetness that gives added depth to this attractive salad.

octopus with roasted pepper,
olives, and sun-dried tomato pesto

Mix the octopus and tentacles in a shallow dish with the olive oil, salt, and pepper.

For the tomato dressing, whisk together all the ingredients until well incorporated. Place the peppers, oven-dried tomatoes, onion, olives, and basil in a large bowl. Pour in the tomato dressing and mix well.

Heat a chargrill until very hot and lay on the octopus and tentacles. Using tongs, toss the octopus continuously to ensure even cooking. Add the cooked octopus to the mizuma leaves, mix well, and place on 4 plates. Spoon a teaspoon of tomato pesto on top of each and serve with the red pepper salad.

you will need

2lbs. baby octopus, tentacles cut in
 half

½ cup olive oil

Salt and freshly ground black pepper

6 tbsp. roasted red bell pepper strips

3 tbsp. oven-dried tomatoes, thinly
 sliced (see page 155)

1 red onion, finely sliced

1½ cups black olives

2 tbsp. basil leaves

2 tbsp. shredded mizuma leaves

6 tsp. sundried tomato pesto

TOMATO DRESSING

1 tbsp. sun-dried tomato paste

2 tbsp. balsamic vinegar

½ cup olive oil

½ tsp. salt

½ tsp. freshly ground black pepper

Serves 4

You will need a large pot for steaming open the mussels, as well as a broiler, but this is still a very quick dish to prepare.

grilled mussels with lemon

and garlic breadcrumbs

you will need

20–30 fresh mussels, scrubbed and rinsed, with beards removed

4 cloves garlic, crushed

2 shallots, roughly chopped

1 stalk lemon grass

2 tbsp. white wine

2 tbsp. water

2 tbsp. chopped parsley

2 tbsp. chopped basil

2 tbsp. chopped cilantro

Grated zest of 1 lemon

3 tbsp. fresh breadcrumbs

⅓ cup olive oil

½ stick (¼ cup) butter, melted

Salt and freshly ground black pepper

Serves 4

Place the mussels in a large pot with half the garlic, the shallots, lemon grass, wine, and water. Cover and steam over high heat for about 5 minutes, or until the shells have opened. Discard any mussels that do not open.

Remove the mussels from their shells, and lay the good mussels in a large heatproof serving dish. Preheat the broiler to high. Mix the remaining garlic with the rest of the ingredients. Spoon this mixture over each mussel and broil until golden and bubbling. Serve immediately with good crusty white bread to mop up all the juices.

Fettuccine Alfredo was one of the first pasta dishes I ever sampled. Pasta was not very popular in Ireland when I was growing up, but fortunately I had an adventurous mother.

you will need

20–30 raw tiger shrimp, shelled and deveined

⅔ cup olive oil

4 tsp. coarse salt

Freshly ground black pepper

1lb. cherry tomatoes, cut in half

1 clove garlic, crushed

Large bunch of fresh parsley, roughly chopped

1lb. dried fettuccine

1 stick (½ cup) butter

Serves 4

fettuccine

with chargrilled shrimp and cherry tomatoes

Place the shrimp in a shallow dish with ¼ cup of the olive oil, 2 teaspoons of coarse salt, and plenty of black pepper. Let it marinate for 1 hour.

Preheat the grill. Drain the shrimp, grill for 2–3 minutes on each side, and remove. Brush the tomatoes with olive oil and place briefly on the grill to heat through. Remove and sprinkle with the garlic and parsley. Season well.

Cook the pasta in plenty of boiling salted water for about 8 minutes, until al dente. Drain and toss with the remaining olive oil and the butter. Add the tomatoes and shrimp, toss well, and serve.

This is one of my favorite dishes, served at Lloyd's Brasserie. Lorcan tried to take it off the menu once, but the customers complained so much that it has returned to stay.

lorcan gribbons's chicken

with piquillo peppers, guacamole, and chile oil

To make the guacamole, mash the avocado with a fork or in a food processor. Mix in the lemon juice, garlic, chile, onion, and chopped cilantro. Season to taste.

Preheat the grill or griddle pan and lightly brush the chicken with some chile oil. Place the chicken strips on the pan and grill for 5 minutes on both sides until the chicken is golden brown.

To serve, spoon some guacamole onto each plate. Top with the lettuce and arrange some chicken and peppers on top. Spoon some more guacamole onto each plate and drizzle with chile oil. Serve immediately.

you will need

4 chicken breasts, skinned and
each one cut into 5 strips

Chile oil

2 heads of romaine lettuce, large leaves
torn in half

1 can Spanish red peppers, drained and
cut in half

1 bunch cilantro

GUACAMOLE

3 ripe avocados, peeled and pitted

Juice of ½ lemon

1 clove garlic, crushed

1 medium chile, seeded and diced

½ medium red onion, diced

½ bunch of cilantro, roughly chopped

Salt and freshly ground black pepper

Serves 4

This was created by chef Gavin and is served at the Metropolitan, Donegal. It incorporates a unique blend of European and Asian flavors.

chargrilled asian chicken

with spiced aïoli and bok choy

you will need

4 chicken breasts, skinned and cut into strips

4 heads bok choy, blanched and refreshed

MARINADE

1 cup corn oil

1-inch piece ginger root, peeled and grated

3 cloves garlic, crushed

½ cup soy sauce

2 tsp. curry powder

2 tsp. honey

Freshly ground black pepper

SPICED AÏOLI

2 egg yolks

2-inch piece ginger root, peeled and grated

2 cloves garlic, crushed

2 tsp. salt

1 tbsp. Dijon mustard

3 tbsp. lime juice

⅓–⅔ cup sunflower oil

Serves 4

Combine all the ingredients for the aïoli in a food processor, except the oil. Leave the machine running and gradually add the oil in a slow steady stream. Add enough oil until the mixture has thickened, then refrigerate until ready to use.

Mix together the marinade ingredients in a shallow dish. Place the chicken strips in the marinade and turn to coat. Leave for at least 40–50 minutes, longer if possible.

Preheat the grill. Lay the chicken strips on it, and chargrill for 5 minutes on each side, then remove. Add the bok choy and grill for 3–4 minutes, turning to grill evenly.

To serve, arrange chicken and bok choy on each plate and drizzle with aïoli.

Quick and simple, but try to allow time to marinate the lamb overnight – it makes all the difference in the world, giving the meat time to absorb the flavors of the herbs.

kebab of lamb

with mediterranean vegetables in pita bread

First make the hummus. Place the drained chickpeas in a food processor with the garlic and olive oil and blend until smooth .

Mix the rosemary, thyme, and garlic with the olive oil in a shallow dish. Add the lamb, turn to coat well, and let it marinate overnight.

Thread the lamb, eggplant, zucchini, and bell pepper on large skewers, alternating meat and vegetables. Grill on a griddle pan or barbecue for about 5 minutes on each side.

Serve with warmed pita bread and hummus on a bed of beansprouts and mesclun, with a spoonful of curried yogurt.

you will need

1 tbsp. chopped rosemary

1 tbsp. chopped thyme

1 clove garlic, crushed

¼ cup olive oil

2½ lb. lamb fillets, trimmed and diced

1 eggplant, diced

1 zucchini, diced

1 red bell pepper, seeded and diced

1 yellow bell pepper, seeded and diced

4 pita breads

½ cup bean sprouts

1 handful of mesclun (gourmet salad mix)

Curried yogurt

Hummus

1 x 14oz. can chickpeas,
    rinsed and drained

2 cloves garlic, crushed

¼ cup olive oil

Serves 4

Figs are one of my favorite fruits. This simple gratin makes the perfect little midnight dessert to finish off dinner after a show.

gratin of figs

with mascarpone

you will need

12 ripe figs

½ cup mascarpone

6 tbsp. fructose (also called fruit sugar and levulose)

3 egg yolks

Juice of 1 lemon

Serves 4

Cut each fig into 5 slices and lay in a broiler pan. Mix the mascarpone with 5 tablespoons of the fructose, the egg yolks, and lemon juice. Spoon into 4 ramekins and sprinkle with the remaining fructose. Place the figs and ramekins under a preheated broiler and cook until the surface of the ramekins is golden brown.

wok

The wok is ideal for one-pot cooking – quick and easy, and almost impossible to get wrong! Once exclusively asian, it is now considered one of the most healthy ways of preparing food. I prefer the round-based wok, since it allows you to cook meat, fish and vegetables rapidly. The wok can also steam – many woks are supplied with steaming racks for this purpose. They should be seasoned before use, and wiped with paper towels after use, not washed.

Being a fatty meat, duck is ideal for cooking at high heat in a wok, the initial stir-frying helping to render out a lot of the fat. Cranberries make a colorful addition – use frozen if fresh are unavailable.

stir-fried duck breast
with fava beans, cranberries, and shiitake

Heat 1 tablespoon of oil in a wok until smoking. Place the duck breasts skin-side down and cook for 1 minute until the fat starts to render out. Remove the breasts from the wok with a slotted spoon and let rest for a few minutes, then slice finely. Wipe the wok clean with paper towels.

Heat the other tablespoon of oil in the wok over medium heat. Add the shallots and sliced duck and stir-fry for 1–2 minutes. Add the shiitake and fresh cranberries. Pour in the chicken stock and simmer until reduced by half. Finally, add the cranberry jelly and fava beans. Cook for 1 more minute and sprinkle with chopped tarragon before serving.

you will need

2 tbsp. vegetable oil

4 duck breasts

3 shallots, sliced

1lb. fresh shiitake mushrooms, sliced

20 fresh cranberries

1¼ cups Chicken Stock (see page153)

2 tbsp. cranberry jelly

1¼ lbs. fresh fava beans, blanched

1 tbsp. chopped tarragon leaves

Serves 4

stir-fried bok choy

with shiitake and ginger

you will need

1 tbsp. olive oil

1lb. bok choy, thinly sliced

½ cup Chicken Stock (see page 153)

2 tbsp. oyster sauce

2 tbsp. soy sauce

2 cloves garlic, crushed

4oz. fresh shiitake mushrooms (about 1 cup)

1-inch piece ginger root, peeled and grated

6 scallions, roughly chopped

1 tbsp. sesame oil

1 tsp. sugar

Salt and freshly ground black pepper

Serves 4

Heat the olive oil in a wok and stir-fry the bok choy until just starting to soften. Add the stock, oyster sauce, and soy sauce. Stir and add the garlic, mushrooms, and ginger. Stir-fry over high heat for 2–3 minutes and then add the remaining ingredients.

Season well and serve.

scallop & shiitake

stir-fry

Heat both the oils in a wok and add the scallops. Toss for a minute, then add the shiitake mushrooms, bok choy stems, and sugar snap peas. Stir-fry for 30 seconds.

Add the ginger, garlic, and bok choy leaves. Add 1–2 tablespoons of water and stir-fry all together for a minute. Add the lime juice and season to taste.

Serve immediately.

you will need

2 tbsp. olive oil

3 tbsp. peanut oil

12 scallops, cut in half

7oz. fresh shiitake mushrooms (about 2 cups)

2 heads baby bok choy, stems and leaves
   sliced separately

40 sugar snap peas, cut in half

1-inch piece ginger root, peeled and chopped

2 cloves garlic, crushed

Juice of 1 lime

Salt and freshly ground black pepper

Serves 4

This elegant confection is delicious, and simple to make, but it does need forward planning as you have to marinate the squid overnight.

soba noodles with soy,

cilantro and marinated squid

you will need

⅔ cup olive oil

1 tbsp. butter

2 limes, sliced

1 stalk lemon grass, chopped

½ bunch of cilantro, chopped

2oz. (3 to 4-inch piece) chopped ginger root

1lb. baby squid, sliced in rings

5oz. soba noodles (available in Asian markets)

3 tbsp. soy sauce

2 tbsp. chopped cilantro

Cilantro leaves, for garnishing

Serves 4

Heat the olive oil and butter in a wok over gentle heat. Add the limes, lemon grass, cilantro, and ginger, and cook for 4 minutes. Remove from heat and stir in the squid. Transfer to a shallow dish and let marinate overnight.

Remove the squid from the marinade with a slotted spoon. Heat 2–3 tablespoons of the marinade in a wok, add the squid, and stir-fry for 3–4 minutes.

Put the soba noodles in a large bowl and pour on enough boiling water to cover. Leave for 30 seconds, then drain and add to the squid. Mix well and add the soy sauce and cilantro. Serve immediately, garnished with cilantro leaves.

The hot, spicy sauce adds a punch to these succulent spring rolls. Everything can be done in the wok, including making the sauce and deep-frying the spring rolls.

crispy spring rolls with duck

and barbecue sauce

To make the barbecue sauce, heat the olive oil in a wok and add all the dry ingredients. Cover and sweat over medium heat for 5 minutes. Add the honey, red wine vinegar, balsamic vinegar, and chicken stock. Bring to a boil and boil until reduced by half, then remove from the heat and transfer to a bowl. Keep warm. Wipe the wok clean with paper towels.

Stir-fry the duck breast in the dry wok over high heat. When the fat starts to render, remove the duck from the wok with a slotted spoon and set aside. Wipe the wok clean with paper towels.

Heat the sesame oil in the wok and add the peppers, carrot, chiles, ginger, garlic, and soy sauce. Stir-fry over high heat for 2–3 minutes, then add the remaining ingredients and the duck. Transfer the filling to a bowl and wipe the wok clean with paper towels.

Brush the spring roll wrappers with the beaten egg. Spoon some of the stir-fried mixture into the center of each one and roll up, tucking in the ends. Heat the oil in the wok to 350°F and deep-fry the spring rolls until golden brown. Remove with a slotted spoon and drain on paper towels. Serve with the barbecue sauce.

you will need

4 spring roll wrappers

1 egg, beaten

Vegetable oil for deep-frying

FILLING

2 duck breasts, thinly sliced

3 tbsp. sesame oil

½ lb. mixed bell peppers, seeded and sliced

1 carrot, sliced

2 chiles, seeded and diced

1-inch piece ginger root, peeled and sliced

1 clove garlic, chopped

1 tbsp. soy sauce

¾ cup sliced sugar snap peas

6 oz. beansprouts (about 3 cups)

2 tbsp. sesame seeds

Zest and juice of 1 lemon, lime and orange

BARBECUE SAUCE

2 tbsp. olive oil

½ lb. mixed bell peppers, seeded and diced

2 tbsp. sesame seeds

2 tbsp. cayenne

1 chile, seeded and diced

4 shallots, diced

⅓ cup honey

2 tbsp. red wine vinegar

2 tsp. balsamic vinegar

1 cup Chicken Stock (see page153)

Serves 4

Another dish that is so simply done. Crab claws can be bought separately and only need a very light cooking.

stir-fried crab claws

with scallions, chile, and garlic

Blend the chile, garlic, and ginger in a food processor until it forms a rough paste. Add the rice wine vinegar, sugar, and salt, and mix well.

Heat the vegetable oil in a wok over medium heat. Add the chile paste and stir-fry for 1–2 minutes. Add the ginger and crab claws. Stir in the fish sauce and add the scallions. Toss well, reduce the heat and place a lid or piece of foil on top. Cook for 2–3 minutes, shaking the wok. Season with black pepper and serve immediately, garnished with scallion strips and cilantro leaves.

you will need

1 red chile, seeded and finely
   chopped

2 cloves garlic, chopped

½-inch piece ginger root, peeled
   and chopped

1½ tbsp. rice wine vinegar

1 tbsp. sugar

½ tsp. sea salt or Kosher salt

½ cup vegetable oil

1 tbsp. chile paste

2oz. ginger root, peeled and sliced
   (3-4 inch piece)

4 crab claws, boiled, shell cracked,
   and cleaned

2 tbsp. naam pla fish sauce

4 scallions, thinly sliced, green
   parts reserved for garnish

Freshly ground black pepper

Cilantro leaves, for garnishing

Serves 2

This recipe enables you to get away from the traditional pork with apple sauce. It has a great Thai flavor, the pork curry blending well with the sweetness of the apples.

pork with cider apples

in a yellow curry with broad beans

you will need

¼ cup vegetable oil

2lbs. pork fillets, finely sliced into strips

3 shallots, sliced

1 stalk lemon grass, sliced

2 yellow bell peppers, seeded and finely sliced

1 tbsp. turmeric

1 tbsp. curry powder

2 Granny Smith apples, quartered and cored

1¼ cups dry cider or, if unavailable, use a

mixture of sweet cider and dry white wine

2½ cups Chicken Stock (see page 153)

1¾lbs. fresh fava beans, blanched until tender

or, if unavailable, peas and/or lima beans

1 tbsp. chopped cilantro

Salt and freshly ground black pepper

Serves 4

Heat half the vegetable oil in a preheated wok over high heat. Add the pork strips and sauté until golden brown in color. Remove the pork from the wok and keep warm.

Wipe out the wok with paper towels, then reheat with the remaining oil. Add the shallots, lemon grass, and peppers, and sauté for 1 minute. Stir in the turmeric and curry power and cook for 1 minute. Add the apples and cook for 2–3 minutes.

Add the cider to the wok and simmer until reduced by half. Add the chicken stock and again simmer until reduced by half. Stir in the broad beans, pork, and chopped cilantro, and season to taste. Serve immediately.

Hot chile jam adds an explosive note to this delicately flavored dish.

stir-fried chicken fillets

with shiitake, sweet potato, and chile jam

Heat the oil in a wok on high heat. Add the chicken and sweet potatoes, and stir-fry for 2–3 minutes. Season with salt and pepper, and add the cilantro.

Add the shiitake mushrooms and stir-fry for 2–3 minutes. Pour in the chicken stock and simmer for 2 minutes, then add the coconut milk and bring to a boil.

Remove from heat and serve in bowls, garnished with chopped cilantro and served with chili jam.

you will need

2 tbsp. olive oil

4 fillets of chicken breast, skinned and finely sliced

1½lbs. sweet potatoes, peeled and grated

Salt and freshly ground black pepper

2 tbsp. chopped cilantro

1lb. fresh shiitake mushrooms, sliced

⅔ cup Chicken Stock (see page 153)

3 tbsp. coconut milk

Chopped cilantro leaves, for garnishing

Chili Jam (see page 155), for serving

Serves 4

baking sheet

In the restaurant trade we refer to baking sheets as *flats*. The low sides mean that food can be easily turned, so the cooking time is greatly reduced. The sheets should be made of aluminum and steel, so that they do not warp at high temperatures, and so that they can withstand direct heat if they have to be placed on the stovetop to finish off a dish, or to sear meat.

This colorful salad, served with Parmesan shavings and garlicky French bread croûtons on top, makes an ideal appetizer.

baby spinach salad

with pancetta, soft-boiled quail eggs, and croûtons

you will need

1 large loaf French bread, sliced

2 cloves garlic, crushed

¼ cup olive oil

Salt and freshly ground black pepper

8 slices pancetta

2 large handfuls baby spinach

¼ cup balsamic vinegar

4 soft-boiled quail eggs, peeled or, if unavailable, small chicken eggs

2 tbsp. sun-dried tomato

½ cup shaved Parmesan

Serves 4

Preheat the oven to 350°F. Rub the bread slices with garlic and place on a baking sheet. Drizzle with the olive oil and season, then bake in the preheated oven for 10 minutes. Place the pancetta on a baking sheet and bake for 1 minute in the oven until crisp.

To serve, toss the spinach with the balsamic vinegar and arrange on a serving dish. Place the baguette slices on top of the spinach. Arrange the eggs, pancetta, sun-dried tomato, and Parmesan shavings on top of the spinach, and serve.

Baked beets are a revelation – sweet and meltingly tender. They make the perfect foil to slices of toasted goat cheese, coated in walnut-flavored breadcrumbs.

baked beets,

goat cheese with walnuts, and arugula

Preheat the oven to 325°F. Wrap each beet in foil and bake in the oven for 1 hour, or until tender. Unwrap and let cool. Leave the oven at the same temperature.

Peel the beets, then them cut into even slices and place in a shallow dish. Add half the vinaigrette, toss to coat, and let marinate.

Peel any rind off the goat cheese and slice it thickly. Brush the cheese with walnut oil and coat each slice with the breadcrumbs. Place the slices on a baking sheet and bake in the oven for 10 minutes to warm the cheese.

Toss the arugula leaves with 1 tablespoon of the vinaigrette. Arrange the leaves in the center of each plate and place some toasted goat cheese on top. Arrange some beets around the plate. Sprinkle with roasted walnuts and drizzle with the remaining vinaigrette.

you will need

1lb. baby beets, trimmed

¼ cup Walnut Vinaigrette (see page 154)

1lb. goat cheese

1 tbsp. walnut oil

3 cups fresh herbed breadcrumbs

8 arugula leaves

1 cup walnuts, oven-roasted

Serves 4

This is ideal for a quick lunch or light dinner, but it would also make a very elegant appetizer, provided the main course is not too heavy.

twice-baked potatoes
with crabmeat and walnuts

Preheat the oven to 350°F. Rinse the potatoes under cold water, wrap in foil and bake in the preheated oven for 1 hour. Remove from the oven and let cool completely. Leave the oven at the same temperature.

Cut off the top of each potato, leaving two-thirds for the base. Scoop out the inside into a bowl, leaving a ¼-inch layer of potato attached to the skin. Add the crème fraîche, herbs, and crabmeat to the potato and mix well. Season to taste with salt and pepper.

Fill each potato with some of the potato mixture. Place on a baking sheet and bake in the preheated oven for 20 minutes, or until golden brown on top. Garnish with fresh herbs and the arugula leaves, and serve on a bed of chopped walnuts and chives.

you will need

4 baking potatoes, about 5oz. each

½ cup crème fraîche or, if unavailable, a mixture of heavy and sour cream

2 tbsp. chopped chives, parsley, or other fresh herbs

4oz. crabmeat (a generous ½ cup)

8 leaves arugula

Salt and freshly ground black pepper

Fresh herb leaves, for garnishing

Chopped walnuts and chives, for serving

Serves 4

This is one of the healthiest ways to cook fish, and also has the advantage of being one of the easiest – it is almost impossible to burn or overcook anything this way.

salmon and leeks

en papillotte

you will need

1 stick (½ cup) butter

4 x 6oz. salmon fillets

2 leeks, finely sliced

¼ cup white wine

¼ cup olive oil

Salt and freshly ground black pepper

2 tbsp. finely chopped chervil

1 tbsp. lemon juice

Serves 4

Preheat the oven to 350°F.

Smear 4 large circles of wax paper or parchment paper with the butter. Place a salmon fillet in the center of each one and top with a quarter of the leeks. Pour a quarter of the white wine and olive oil over each fillet and season well. Add the chervil, then draw up the edges of the paper to seal the packets.

Place the packets on a baking sheet and cook in the oven for about 10–15 minutes, depending on how well done you like the salmon. Carefully unwrap the packets so that you do not get burned from the steam, and try to retain as much of the juice as possible. Place each fillet on a plate and spoon some of the leek mixture on top. Serve immediately, sprinkled with lemon juice.

There are many variations of this delicious galette that you can try, such as using sliced zucchini insead of tomatoes, and arugula instead of mixed herbs – whatever takes your fancy.

baked tomato

and tapenade galette

Warm the goat cheese and cream in a small pan and mix until well combined. Remove from heat and add pepper and the chopped basil. Set aside.

you will need

4 x 6-inch circles of puff pastry, ½ inch thick

¼ cup Sun-dried Tomato Tapenade (see page 155)

8 medium plum tomatoes

¼ cup Tomato Oil (see page 152)

Salt and freshly ground black pepper

Selection of chopped fresh herbs, such as chives, parsley, chervil and basil

¼ cup balsamic vinegar

GOAT CHEESE MIXTURE

10oz. goat cheese, chopped

½ cup heavy cream

Freshly ground black pepper

2 tbsp. chopped basil

Serves 4

Preheat the oven to 350°F. Place the puff pastry circles between 2 sheets of wax paper and place on a baking sheet. Lay another baking sheet on top (to ensure that the pastry won't rise), and bake for 15 minutes. Remove from the oven and let cool on a wire rack. Turn down the oven to a low temperature.

Spread the pastry circles with the sun dried tomato tapenade. Spoon a small amount of the goat cheese mixture into the center of each circle. Slice the plum tomatoes thinly and arrange on top. Drizzle the circles with tomato oil, season with salt and pepper, and put in a low oven to warm for 3–4 minutes.

Serve sprinkled with fresh herbs, and drizzled with balsamic vinegar.

The tangy cheese perfectly balances the richness of the ham in these exciting packages, served on a bed of mixed salad greens.

baked goat cheese

with prosciutto

you will need

13oz. hard goat cheese

4 large slices prosciutto

4 basil leaves

Freshly ground black pepper

2 tbsp. olive oil

Mixed salad greens, for serving

Serves 4

Preheat the oven to 400°F.

Remove the rind from the goat cheese and cut into 4 slices.
Lay out the prosciutto and place a basil leaf in the center of each piece. Place a slice of goat cheese on top and season with black pepper. Wrap up neatly in the prosciutto, then tightly wrap in plastic. Chill for about 1 hour.

Remove the plastic wrap from the packages and place them on a baking sheet. Drizzle with olive oil and bake in the preheated oven for 10 minutes. The prosciutto should just start to crisp.

Serve with mixed salad greens.

This pizza is simple enough to prepare, the oven-dried tomatoes adding a delicious sweetness to the topping.

white cheese pizza

with artichoke, arugula, and oven-dried tomatoes

To make the dough, mix all the dry ingredients in a food processor. Mix the water and yeast and gradually add to the flour on a medium speed for 10 minutes, until a smooth dough is formed.

you will need

6 cloves garlic, unskinned

1 tbsp. olive oil

1 recipe Oven-dried Tomatoes
(see page 155)

⅛lb. arugula

1 can artichoke hearts, drained

1¾lbs. buffalo mozzarella, sliced

PIZZA DOUGH

4 cups all-purpose flour

1 tsp. salt

Pinch of sugar

2 cups warm water

2 tsp. fresh yeast

Serves 4

Shape the pizza dough into 4 very thin discs on a greased baking sheet and let them rest for 30 minutes. Preheat the oven to 350°F. Place the garlic on a baking sheet, sprinkle with the olive oil, and roast for 10 minutes. Remove the garlic from its skins.

Bake the pizza bases in the preheated oven for 20 minutes. Remove from the oven and reduce the temperature to 325°F.

Spread the dried tomatoes over the bases and cover with arugula. Arrange the artichokes on top and sprinkle with the peeled roast garlic. Place slices of mozzarella on top and sprinkle with olive oil. Return the pizzas to the oven for 20 minutes.

You can make lots of variations on this theme, using shrimp, scallops, or artichokes instead of the chorizo, for example, and mozzarella or blue cheese in place of the goat cheese.

tomato & goat cheese pizza

with chorizo and arugula

you will need

1 quantity recipe Pizza Dough (see page 123)

6 ripe plum tomatoes, sliced

1 x 4oz. log of goat cheese, sliced,
plus extra for sprinkling

20 thin slices of chorizo (about 4oz.)

Coarse salt and freshly ground black pepper

1lb. arugula

¼ cup olive oil

Serves 4

Shape the pizza dough into 4 very thin discs on a greased baking sheet. Let them rest for 30 minutes. Preheat the oven to 350°F.

Bake the pizza bases for 20 minutes in the preheated oven, then remove from the heat and let cool. Reduce the oven temperature to 325°F.

Cover the bases with alternate layers of tomatoes, goat cheese, and chorizo. Season with coarse salt and black pepper and bake in the preheated oven until the cheese has melted, about 10 minutes.

Toss the arugula with the olive oil and season. Serve the pizza with the arugula piled on top.

I love eating chocolate with coffee, and these cookies and muffins make perfect petit fours. Both are simple to make and store perfectly.

chunky chocolate cookies

Preheat the oven to 375°F. Lightly grease 2 baking sheets.

you will need

½ stick (¼ cup) lightly salted butter, plus extra for greasing

1¼ cups all-purpose flour

½ tsp. baking soda

1¼ cups plus 2 tbsp. sugar

1 tsp. vanilla essence

1 egg, beaten

6oz. dark or milk chocolate, chopped into small pieces (about 2 cups)

4oz. white chocolate, chopped into small pieces (about 1⅓ cups)

Turbinado or brown sugar

Serves 20

Melt the butter in a small pan, then let cool slightly. Sift the flour and baking soda into a bowl. Add the sugar, melted butter, vanilla, and egg. Stir in the chocolate. Using a large spoon, place spoonfuls of the mixture on the baking sheets, spacing them well apart, and sprinkle with the turbinado or brown sugar.

Bake the cookies for about 15 minutes until golden around the edges. Remove from the oven and leave on the baking sheet for 5 minutes, then transfer to a wire rack to cool.

mini chocolate muffins

Preheat the oven to 325°F.

Place the egg, butter, and vanilla in a bowl and beat well together. Sift the flour, salt, and baking powder into the bowl. Stir in the brown sugar, then add the milk and lightly fold in with a metal spoon. Do not over-mix. Stir in the chocolate.

Spoon the mixture into a buttered mini muffin sheet. Sprinkle with the light brown sugar and bake for 10 minutes until risen. Cool on a wire rack.

you will need

1 egg, beaten

3 tbsp. melted butter, plus extra for greasing

Few drops of vanilla extract

¾ cup plus 2 tbsp. self-rising flour

Pinch of salt

½ tsp. baking powder

3 tbsp. brown sugar

¼ cup milk

⅔ cup chopped white chocolate

2 tbsp. light brown sugar

Serves 20

You could also flavor the bread with other herbs, such as thyme or rosemary. Bread recipes usually tell you to leave the dough to rise in a warm place, but in fact it is best to let it rise slowly at room temperature.

sun-dried tomato
and basil bread

In a food processor, mix together the flour and salt. Cream the yeast with the sugar and 1–2 tablespoons of the warm water. Mix the remaining water with the tomato paste and add to the flour along with the yeast mixture, sun-dried tomatoes, basil, and olive oil. Process until the dough comes together and feels quite soft but not sticky. Add more water if necessary.

Turn the dough out onto a lightly floured surface and knead until smooth and elastic, about 10 minutes. Place the dough in a lightly greased bowl, cover with a clean dish towel and let rise at room temperature for 1½–2 hours, until doubled in size.

Punch down the dough and shape into a long loaf. Place the dough on a baking sheet, cover with a clean, damp dish towel, and let it rise for 1½–2 hours until doubled in size. Preheat the oven to 400°F.

Dust the loaf with flour and sprinkle with a little water. Bake in the preheated oven for 15 minutes, then reduce the temperature to 350°F. Bake for another 25 minutes, or until the loaf sounds hollow when tapped on the bottom. Remove from the baking sheet and let it cool on a wire rack.

you will need

6 cups all-purpose flour

1 tsp. salt

1tbsp. fresh yeast or fast-action dried yeast

1 tsp. sugar

1¼ cups warm water

¼ cup tomato paste

7oz. sun-dried tomatoes in olive oil, drained and
   finely chopped (1 generous cup)

1 tbsp. finely chopped basil

¼ cup olive oil

Makes 1 large loaf

Make the sorbet in advance and store in the freezer.

mango sorbet

with tuiles

Heat the water and sugar in a small pan over gentle heat until the sugar dissolves. Once the sugar has dissolved, bring to a boil, then simmer for 5 minutes. Let cool slightly, then stir into the mango purée and mix well. Pour into a freezer container and freeze until ready to use.

Preheat the oven to 350°F. Line a baking sheet with wax paper or parchment paper.

To make the tuiles, whip the butter and sugar until light and creamy, then fold in the flour, being careful not to over-mix. Place spoonfuls of the batter on the baking sheet, then spread it out as thinly as possible with the back of a spoon.

Bake in the preheated oven for 10 minutes, then remove with a spatula while still hot and shape by molding each one round a champagne or other bottle. Leave in position to cool, then fill with sorbet when cold.

you will need

⅔ cup water

2 tbsp. sugar

1¼ cups puréed mango, strained

TUILES

2½ sticks (1¼ cups) butter

1¼ cups sugar

1¾ cups self-rising flour

Serves 4

This is ideal for a delicious dessert provided the main course is not too heavy.

lemon tart

Preheat the oven to 325°F.

To make the pastry, combine the butter, sugar, and flour together in a food processor. Add the two eggs and mix to make a smooth dough. Wrap the dough in plastic wrap and chill for at least 30 minutes before using.

Roll out the pastry and use to line one 8-inch greased fluted tart pan, or 4 individual tart pans. Transfer to the freezer for 20 minutes. Bake straight from the freezer for 10 minutes, or until golden brown. Remove from the oven and let cool. Reduce the oven temperature to 225°F.

To make the filling, bring the cream and lemon zest to a boil in a pan. Combine the sugar, egg yolks, and lemon juice in a bowl. Whisk the cream mixture into the egg mixture, combining thoroughly. Strain the filling into the tart shell and bake for 20–30 minutes.

you will need

3¾ sticks butter (2 cups minus 2 tbsp.)

1 cup sugar

5 cups self-rising flour

2 eggs

FILLING

2 pints heavy cream

Zest and juice of 7 lemons

¾ cups plus 2 tbsp. sugar

10 egg yolks

Serves 4

baking dish

The most useful baking dishes are flameproof, so that cooking can be started off on top of the stove, if need be. Dishes come in all shapes and sizes, from the large, oval, or rectangular kind used to cook baked pasta, apple crumble, and similar dishes, to the small individual ramekins or soufflé dishes used for elegant desserts such as crème brûlée.

Squid baked in a Provençal-style sauce is tender and full of flavor.

provençal-style baked squid

with rice pilaf

you will need

4 medium squid tubes

⅔ cup ground almonds

STUFFING

¼ cup olive oil

1 onion, chopped

4 cloves garlic, finely chopped

¾ cup short-grain Italian brown rice

1¼ cups water

1 bunch of parsley, chopped

4 sprigs oregano, chopped

Salt and freshly ground pepper

TOMATO AND PEPPER SAUCE

½ cup olive oil

1 onion, sliced

2 cloves garlic, sliced

2 zucchini, sliced

2 red bell peppers, seeded and sliced

14 oz. can of tomatoes

1 bay leaf

3 sprigs thyme

1 cup water

Salt and freshly ground black pepper

Serves 4

Preheat the oven to 400°F.

To make the sauce, heat the olive oil in a flameproof baking dish over medium heat, add the onion and garlic, cover, and sweat for 3 minutes. Add the zucchini and peppers, and sweat for another 3 minutes. Add the tomatoes and their juices, the herbs and water. Bring to a boil and simmer gently for 5 minutes. Season with salt and pepper and remove from heat. Transfer the sauce to a bowl and rinse out the dish.

To cook the stuffing, heat the olive oil in the dish over medium heat, add the onion and garlic, cover, and sweat for 3 minutes. Add the rice, cover and sweat again for 2 minutes. Pour in the water and cook over medium heat for 30 minutes, or until the rice has absorbed all the water.

Mix half the parsley with the rice, add the oregano, and season. Stuff the rice mixture into the squid tubes and close the ends with skewers. Pour the tomato sauce into the baking dish and place the stuffed squid on top. Sprinkle with the ground almonds and remaining parsley, and bake in the preheated oven for 15–20 minutes. Serve the squid with the sauce spooned on top.

The meaty flesh of monkfish, spiked with garlic, also goes well with the fruity flavors of the Provençal-style sauce.

gigot of monkfish

Preheat the oven to 350°F.

Make 3 incisions with a sharp knife across the back of each piece of monkfish.
Insert half a garlic clove into each incision.

Make the sauce in a flameproof baking dish. Place the monkfish on top of the sauce and pour the olive oil over the monkfish. Transfer to the preheated oven and cook for 15 minutes.

To serve, spoon some sauce on each plate and place a piece of monkfish in the center.

you will need

4 X 7oz. monkfish tails

6 cloves garlic, cut in half

¼ cup olive oil

Tomato and Pepper Sauce (see page 134)

Baked eggplant has a wonderful smoky flavor and a softly melting texture.

marinated eggplant salad

with baked chicken

Preheat the oven to 350°F. Place the eggplants in a large flameproof baking dish. Pour the olive oil over them and sprinkle with the garlic, balsamic vinegar, and thyme. Season well and cook for 30–40 minutes until tender, turning the eggplants half-way through cooking. Remove from the oven, transfer to a serving dish and keep warm. Increase the temperature to 400°F.

Heat the sunflower oil in the baking dish. Season the chicken breasts and add to the dish. Sear on both sides, then add the butter. Transfer the dish to the oven to finish cooking, about 7–10 minutes.

Reheat the eggplants if necessary, and serve with the chicken breasts.

you will need

6 eggplants, cubed

⅔ cup olive oil

2 cloves garlic, crushed

¼ cup balsamic vinegar

1 tsp. chopped thyme

Salt and freshly ground black pepper

2 tbsp. sunflower oil or other vegetabe oil

4 chicken breasts

½ stick (¼ cup) butter

Serves 4

you will need

4–6 plums

¼ cup puréed passion fruit

½ tsp. star anise

½ tsp. ground cinnamon

3 tbsp. butter, diced

2 tbsp. sugar

CRÈME CHANTILLY

1¼ cups heavy cream

1 vanilla bean, split and seeds removed

¼ cup confectioners sugar

Serves 4

This is so simple, and cooks in a few minutes, yet it looks and tastes heavenly. What more could you want?

baked spiced plums

with herbs and crème chantilly

Preheat the oven to 375°F.

Cut the plums in half and remove the pits. Place the plums , skin-side down, in an ovenproof dish and drizzle with the passion fruit purée. Sprinkle the spices, butter, and sugar on top, and bake in the preheated oven for 10 minutes.

Remove from the oven and baste with the cooking juices. Lightly whip the cream and fold in the vanilla seeds and confectioners sugar. Serve the crumble with a spoonful of the crème chantilly on top.

The brûlée is topped with a layer of crisp caramel, with creamy custard and raspberries hidden underneath.

raspberry & mascarpone

with a layer of crisp caramel

you will need

3 egg yolks

2 eggs

¼ cup sugar

1 cup milk

1 cup heavy cream

2 vanilla beans, split and seeds removed

⅓ cup mascarpone

1¼-1½ cups raspberries, plus a few extra

for decoration

⅓ cup sugar

Serves 4

Preheat the oven to 250°F.

Whisk the egg yolks and eggs in a bowl with the sugar until pale and creamy. Heat the milk and cream over gentle heat and slowly pour into the egg mixture. Strain through a fine sieve and then scrape in the vanilla seeds. While the mixture is still warm, add the mascarpone and mix well.

Place the raspberries in the bottom of 4 ramekins and pour in the custard. Place the ramekins in a baking dish and half-fill with water. Place in the oven and cook for 30–40 minutes. Remove from the heat and let cool.

To finish, sprinkle each ramekin with a layer of sugar and glaze under a broiler until the sugar melts and caramelizes. Let cool, then decorate with a few fresh raspberries.

The sweet-sour lime sauce, with its hint of acidity, is the perfect complement to this heavenly sweet mango soufflé.

mango soufflé

with lime sabayon

you will need

4–6 mangoes, peeled and diced

¼ cup water

Juice and zest of 3 limes

5 egg whites

¼ cup sugar, plus extra for dusting

butter for greasing

LIME SAUCE

3 limes

3 tbsp. light brown sugar

2 tbsp. sweet butter

1 cup heavy cream

Serves 4

Put the mangoes in a pan with the water and place over gentle heat.
Simmer for 5 minutes. Add the lime juice and zest.
Purée in a food processor and set aside.

Preheat the oven to 350°F.

Beat the egg whites in a large bowl and gently add the sugar.
With a metal spoon, fold the mango purée into the egg mixture.
Butter 4 medium-sized soufflé dishes and dust with sugar, making sure the dishes are completely coated. Gently pour in the mango mixture and lightly smooth the top.
Cook the soufflés for 25 minutes, or until the top has browned and risen.

For the sauce, grate the rind of 2 limes. Mix the zest with the juice of all 3 limes and pour into a small pan. Add the brown sugar and cook over low heat until the sugar has dissolved. Add the butter and let it melt, then pour in the cream and stir thoroughly. Bring the sauce to a boil, and let it bubble for 2 minutes until the cream has thickened. Pour the sauce into a pitcher or gravy boat.

Serve the soufflés the moment they are ready, with the sauce.

Crumble is one of my all-time favorite desserts. Served with cream or ice cream, it makes heavenly winter fare.

raisin, pear, & apple crumble

you will need

2 Granny Smith apples, peeled, cored, and finely diced

2 pears, peeled, cored, and finely diced

⅓ cup raisins

2 tbsp. Cointreau

3 tbsp. sugar

Pinch of ground cinnamon

1¾ cups flour

1 stick (½ cup) butter, cut into cubes and chilled

¼ cup light brown sugar

Whipping cream or ice cream, for serving

Serves 4

Preheat the oven to 350°F.

Mix together the apples, pears, raisins, Cointreau, sugar, and cinnamon in a bowl. Chill until ready to use.

Sift the flour into a bowl and rub in the butter until the mixture resembles breadcrumbs. Mix in the brown sugar. Fill 4 individual ramekins or 1 large one with the fruit mixture, and top with crumble mixture. Bake for about 30 minutes, until the fruit is soft and the crumble topping is starting to color.

Serve with fresh cream or ice cream.

deep fryer

Abused by images of a smoking French fry pan and the smell of stale oil, the deep fryer needs some serious PR. The traditional deep fryer is made of stainless steel, with handles on either side. A basket with long handles allows you to lower food into the fat for rapid cooking at high temperatures. Deep fryers bring out the best in savory pastries – the goat cheese wontons are cooked to perfection, the cheese molten, the pastry crisp, and not a French fry in sight.

Crisp deep-fried wontons enhance this elegant, piquantly flavored salad.

spicy asian salad

with goat cheese wontons

Mix the cabbage, carrot, pepper, and ginger in a bowl.

In another bowl mix the soy sauce, peanut butter, sugar, lime juice, and chile. Add to the cabbage mixture, mix well, and let marinate for 3 hours.

Drain the salad and mix the goat cheese with the liquid. Place a teaspoon of the mixture on each wonton skin, wet the edges, and gather together to make little packets.

Heat the oil for deep-frying to 350°F in a large pot or deep fryer. Add the wontons and deep-fry for 2–3 minutes, until golden brown.

Serve the wontons with the salad and garnish with cilantro.

you will need

¼lb. green cabbage, shredded finely
(about 3½-4 cups)

1 small carrot, cut into long fine strips

1 red bell pepper, seeded and cut into long
fine strips

2 tbsp. ground ginger

¼ cup soy sauce

1 tbsp. peanut butter

1 tbsp. sugar

2 tbsp. lime juice

½ tbsp. chopped and seeded chile

1 packet wonton skins (available from
specialist stores)

¼lb. goat cheese, crumbled (about ½ cup)

Vegetable oil for deep-frying

¼ cup cilantro leaves

Serves 4

Ideal party or buffet fare, or for dinner guests to dip into while you get on with the serious cooking. It can all be prepared ahead of time.

mini crabcakes

with dips and asian slaw

Flake the crabmeat into a bowl. Mix with the remaining ingredients and season well. Roll the mixture into small balls, about ½-inch in diameter, and chill for 2–3 hours.

Heat the oil in a deep-fryer to 350°F. Deep-fry the cakes until golden brown, then remove with a slotted spoon. Drain on paper towels and sprinkle with salt.

Mix all the dips in separate dishes or bowls. Place the slaw ingredients in a salad bowl. Mix together the dressing ingredients and pour them over the salad. Toss well. Serve the crabcakes with the dips and salad.

you will need

12oz. white crabmeat

2 tbsp. finely chopped cilantro

1 tbsp. finely chopped parsley

Zest and juice of 2 lemons

2 tbsp. heavy cream

2 egg yolks

1½ cups fresh white breadcrumbs

Salt and freshly ground black pepper

Vegetable oil, for deep-frying

DRESSING

⅔ cup olive oil

¼ cup sesame oil

¼ cup soy sauce

¼ cup rice vinegar

2 tbsp. sugar

Juice of 1 lime

Salt and freshly ground black pepper

SESAME DIP

¼ cup sesame oil

¼ cup peanut oil

3 tbsp. honey

2 tbsp. soy sauce

3 tbsp. hoisin sauce

ASIAN SLAW

2 heads bok choy, sliced and

blanched

1 small radiccio lettuce, finely sliced

½ head iceberg lettuce, very

finely sliced

3 papaya, peeled and

roughly chopped

2 tsp. roasted sesame seeds

BARBECUE DIP

3 tbsp. ketchup

3 tbsp. barbecue sauce

1 tbsp. honey

3 tbsp. soy sauce

1 tbsp. Worcestershire sauce

2 tbsp. Dijon mustard

HONEY AND SOY DIP

6 tbsp. soy sauce

2 tbsp. honey

1 tbsp. lime juice

A filling, tasty Chinese soup which makes a meal in itself. You can make it all in one pan, or you could deep-fry the wontons separately.

chile beef with broth

and goat cheese dumplings

Heat a large pan over high heat until at smoking point, then add the olive oil. Add the beef, sear on all sides, then remove from the pan with a slotted spoon.

Add all the vegetables to the pan and sauté for 2–3 minutes. Add the thyme, rosemary, and vegetable stock. Bring to a boil and cook for about 10 minutes, or until all the vegetables are tender. Return the beef to the broth and stir in the Chinese cabbage, beansprouts, cilantro, and parsley. Simmer for a few minutes, then transfer the soup to a bowl and keep warm. Rinse out the pan.

To make the dumplings, place a ball of goat cheese in the center of each wonton wrapper. Brush the edges with beaten egg and gather up to make small bags. Deep-fry at 350°F for 30 seconds until crisp, then drain on paper towels.

Rinse out the pan, then return the soup to the pan to heat through. Serve the soup in a large bowl with the dumplings on top.

you will need

½ cup olive oil

2lbs. sirloin beef, thinly sliced

3 chiles, seeded and finely diced

5 shallots, finely sliced

1 zucchini, finely diced

2 cloves garlic, finely diced

1 large potato, finely diced

1 large carrot, finely diced

1 tbsp. chopped rosemary

1 tbsp. thyme leaves

2 quarts Vegetable Stock
   (see page 153)

2 heads Chinese cabbage, chopped

2 cups beansprouts

2 tbsp. cilantro leaves

2 tbsp. flat-leaf parsley

Salt and freshly ground black pepper

GOAT CHEESE DUMPLINGS

8 wonton skins (available from Asian markets)

8 small balls of goat cheese

1 egg, whisked with a little salt

Vegetable oil, for deep-frying

Serves 6

These tasty "sandwiches", using deep-fried eggplant slices in place of bread and with a cheese and salad filling, make a very attractive appetizer, or a quick lunch-time snack.

eggplant, goat cheese

and pesto sandwich

you will need

3 medium eggplants

Salt

Vegetable oil, for deep frying

2 tbsp. balsamic vinegar

⅛ cup virgin olive oil

Freshly ground black pepper

10oz. goat cheese, cut into ½-inch thick slices

2 red bell peppers, seeded and cut in strips

3 tbsp. Basil Pesto (see page 155)

3 tbsp. finely shredded arugula leaves

Serves 6

Cut the eggplants into thick slices and sprinkle with salt. Leave on a tray for 1 hour, then dry with paper towels to remove the salt.

Heat the oil in a deep-fryer to 350°F and fry the eggplant slices until golden brown. Remove with a slotted spoon and drain on paper towels.

Make a vinaigrette by whisking together the balsamic vinegar, olive oil, salt, and pepper.

To make each sandwich, place a slice of eggplant on a plate and top with a slice of goat cheese. Cover the cheese with some of the pepper strips, then add a teaspoon of pesto. Drizzle with vinaigrette and sprinkle with arugula.

salads, etc.

The salad is one of the simplest concepts in cooking, the salad bowl being the perfect *pot* for recipes that are prepared in minutes. Of course, a salad's success lies in its dressing, so I have included a host of oils, vinaigrettes, and dressings to make even a simple green salad a delight. This chapter also includes stocks, sauces, and accompaniments that are certainly not difficult, but will give your dishes that much-desired professional touch.

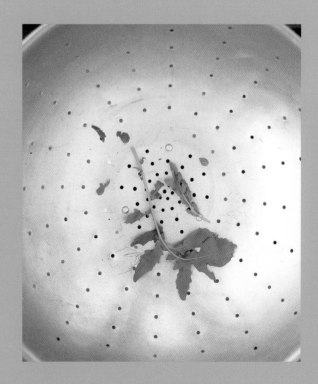

thai salad with nori, beans, and lime dressing

2 tbsp. pickled ginger

4 red salad onions, finely sliced

4 Garlic Confit (see page 157)

1 tbsp. coconut shavings, toasted

2 sprigs cilantro

2 sprigs chervil

2oz. chives (about 2 handfuls)

4 chicken breasts, cooked and diced

1 chile, seeded and finely diced

2 cups beansprouts

2oz. anchovies, chopped (about ⅓ cup)

2 romaine lettuce leaves, shredded

4 nori seaweed sheets, shredded finely

1 scallion, chopped

DRESSING

Zest and juice of 2 limes

¼ cup olive oil

Salt and freshly ground black pepper

PICKLED CUCUMBER

1 cucumber, peeled, seeded and diced

4 tsp. sesame oil

1 tsp. sesame seeds

1 tsp. white wine

1 tsp. white wine vinegar

½ tsp. malt vinegar

2 tbsp. honey

Serves 4

To make the pickled cucumber, place the sesame oil, sesame seeds, white wine, vinegars, and honey in a small pan and bring to a boil. Add the cucumber and remove from the heat. Let cool.

Place all the salad ingredients in a large bowl with 2 tbsp. of the pickled cucumber and toss well.

To make the dressing, mix the lime zest and juice with the olive oil, and season with salt and pepper. Pour the dressing over the salad and let marinate for 1 hour.

fennel salad with red apple, chile, and mustard

4 fennel bulbs

1lb. asparagus spears

1 eating apple, cored and diced

1½ cups chopped chives

1½ cups chopped cilantro

1 chile, seeded and diced

Juice and zest of 1 lemon

2 tbsp. sugar

½lb. arugula

¼lb. romaine lettuce (about 1½ cups)

2 shallots, diced

¼ cup Balsamic Vinaigrette (see page 154)

1 tbsp. grated Parmesan

Salt and freshly ground black pepper

¼ cup chile oil

Serves 4

Blanch the fennel and asparagus in a large pot of boiling water, drain, refresh under cold water, and drain again. Slice the fennel finely.

Mix the apple, chives, cilantro, chile, lemon zest, juice, and sugar in a bowl. Add the arugula, romaine lettuce, shallots, and dressing, and toss well. Add the Parmesan and season. Arrange the salad in the center of a large plate. Lay the asparagus and fennel on top and drizzle with chile oil.

mixed bean salad with feta cheese and pita bread

1 cup canned flageolet beans

1 cup canned (or cooked) black-eyed beans

1 cup canned lima beans

1 cup canned borlotti beans

Salt and freshly ground black pepper

¼lb. feta, chopped (about 1 cup)

20 cherry tomatoes

½ bunch Italian parsley (flat leaf)

1⅓ cups marinated black olives

Chopped flat-leaf parsley, for garnishing

DRESSING

½ cup olive oil

2 shallots, finely chopped

2 sprigs thyme, leaves removed

Juice of 2 lemons

Serves 4

Drain all the beans, place in a large bowl, and season with salt and pepper. Mix in all the remaining ingredients. Mix the vinaigrette ingredients together, add to the bowl, and toss well. Garnish with flat-leaf parsley. Serve with grilled warm pita bread on the side.

Season and chill. Mix the vegetables and olive oil and let marinate for 10 minutes.

green salad

3 heads corn salad or, if unavailable, salad greens

½lb. arugula (4-5 cups)

Small bunch of tarragon

Small bunch of basil

Small bunch of cilantro

Small bunch of chervil

Small bunch of chives, roughly chopped

½ head red oak or red leaf lettuce

Balsamic Vinaigrette (see page 154) or other dressing

Serves 4

Wash and dry all lettuce and herbs and toss with your favorite dressing. The balsamic vinaigrette goes best with this.

flavoured oils

chile oil

1¼ cups olive oil

2 carrots, finely diced

2 onions, finely diced

3 celery stalks, finely chopped

1 leek, finely chopped

1 clove garlic, chopped

2 sprigs thyme

1 sprig rosemary

1lb. red chiles, seeded and chopped

1lb. red bell peppers, seeded and chopped

3 tbsp. tomato paste

Salt

Heat 3 tablespoons of the olive oil in a heavy pan over medium heat. Add the vegetables, herbs, chiles, and peppers, cover, and sweat for 5–10 minutes. Add the tomato paste, mix well, and cook for 2 minutes. Stir in the remaining olive oil and cook on low heat until all the vegetables are tender, about 20 minutes. Season with salt, remove from heat, and let cool in the pan. When cool, strain through a fine sieve. Store refrigerated for 3 days .

dill oil

2 cups dill, finely chopped

1 cup olive oil

Juice of 1 lemon

Salt and freshly ground black pepper

Mix all the ingredients together and store for 2–3 days in the refrigerator.

basil oil

2 cups basil leaves

1–2 tbsp. water

1 cup olive oil

Salt and freshly ground black pepper

1 clove garlic, crushed

Purée the basil with the water in a food processor. Do this quickly, because if you process the basil for too long it will lose its bright color. Transfer to a bowl and gradually whisk in the oil. Season and add the garlic. Refrigerate for up to 3 days.

tomato oil

1 cup olive oil

2 cloves garlic, crushed

2 shallots, chopped

1 celery stalk, chopped

¼ fennel bulb, chopped

1 tbsp. chopped basil

½ tbsp. chopped oregano

2 bay leaves

3 tbsp. tomato paste

Salt and freshly ground black pepper

Heat 1 tablespoon of olive oil in a medium-sized pan and add the garlic, shallots, celery, fennel, basil, oregano, and bay leaves. Cover and sweat for 5 minutes over medium heat until the vegetables are tender, but not colored. Add the tomato paste and mix well. Continue to cook gently for another 10 minutes, making sure the heat is very low, as the mixture is quite dry and could burn easily. Gradually add the remaining oil, stirring continuously. Season well and cook gently for another 1½–2 hours.

Let cool, then strain the mixture through a fine sieve. The oil will have separated from the sediment. For an extra clear oil, strain twice though cheesecloth. Adjust the seasoning if necessary. Store refrigerated for 2–3 days.

beetroot oil

4 beets, peeled

Salt and freshly ground black pepper

2 tbsp. balsamic vinegar

1 tsp. sugar

½ cup olive oil

This is only practical to make when you are cooking beets anyway.

Cook the beets in boiling salted water until tender (about 40-50 minutes), then drain, reserving the liquid. Place the liquid in a pan with the vinegar and sugar, and boil until reduced by half. Let cool, then whisk in the olive oil. Season and refrigerate for up to 2–3 days.

curry oil

2 cloves garlic, roughly chopped

2 shallots, roughly chopped

2 sprigs thyme

3 tbsp. curry powder

1 tsp. ground cumin

1 tsp. fennel seeds, crushed

Salt and freshly ground black pepper

1¼ cups olive oil

Preheat the oven to 300°F.

Place all the dry ingredients in a roasting pan. Pour ½ cup of the olive oil over them and roast for 1 hour. Transfer the ingredients to a medium-sized pan along with the remaining oil and cook over gentle heat for 2 hours. Remove from heat and let cool overnight. Strain, then store refrigerated for 2–3 days.

stocks

chicken stock

Makes about 1 quart

4lbs. raw chicken bones or carcasses

3 quarts cold water

1 leek, roughly chopped

1 carrot, roughly chopped

1 onion, unpeeled, roughly chopped

1 sprig rosemary

Salt and freshly ground black pepper

Place the bones in a large pot and add the water. Bring to a boil, skimming off any impurities on the surface. Add the remaining ingredients. Bring to a boil once more, then reduce the heat and simmer gently for at least 4 hours. Skim the stock regularly.

Let cool slightly, then remove the bones. Strain through a fine sieve or preferably cheesecloth. Discard the vegetables and bones. Reduce the stock by rapid boiling if it lacks flavor. Otherwise let it cool down, and then refrigerate or freeze it.

beef or veal stock

Makes about 2 quarts

4lbs. beef or veal bones

½ cup olive oil

Salt and freshly ground black pepper

1 large onion, unpeeled and roughly chopped

2 shallots, unpeeled and roughly chopped

2 large carrots, roughly chopped

2 celery stalks, roughly chopped

4 cloves garlic, chopped

½ bottle red wine

8 quarts cold water

1 bay leaf

1 sprig thyme

Preheat the oven to 400°F. Place the bones in a large roasting pan. Brush with 1 cup of the olive oil and season well. Roast in the oven for up to 2 hours until very well browned.

Heat the remaining olive oil in a very large pot, and sauté the onion, shallots, carrots, celery, and garlic until well browned. Add the red wine and simmer until reduced by half. Add the water, mix well, and add the bones. Bring to a boil and simmer uncovered for at least 4 hours, skimming off any fat or impurities that rise to the surface. Add more water if necessary, as the bones must be kept covered.

Remove the bones, strain the stock through a colander and then through cheesecloth or a fine sieve. Transfer to a clean pot and boil until reduced by at least half. Let cool and reheat or freeze as required.

lamb stock

Makes 2 cups

2 tbsp. olive oil

2lbs. lamb bones

10 shallots, roughly chopped

Salt and freshly ground black pepper

2 cloves garlic, crushed

1 tbsp. grated fresh horseradish

1 tbsp. tomato paste

½ tsp. chopped tarragon

2 sprigs rosemary

1½ quarts Chicken Stock (see left) or water

Preheat the oven to 400°F. Pour 1 tablespoon of olive oil into a large roasting pan. Add the bones and roast in the oven until well browned, about 40 minutes. Turn the bones occasionally to ensure an even color.

Meanwhile, heat the remaining olive oil in a large pot and sauté the shallots. Season with a little salt and pepper. When the shallots have browned evenly, add the garlic, horseradish, and tomato paste. Cook for a further 5 minutes and then add the herbs, stock, or water, and the bones. Bring to a boil, then reduce the heat and simmer for 3 hours. Skim the stock regularly to remove any fat or impurities that rise to the surface. When the stock is ready, remove the bones and strain the stock through a fine sieve or cheesecloth 3 times. Transfer to a clean pot, and boil until reduced to about half. Let it cool down, then refrigerate or freeze.

vegetable stock

Makes 2 cups

½ stick (¼ cup) butter

2 zucchinis, roughly chopped

2 leeks, roughly chopped

2 carrots, roughly chopped

2 celery stalks, roughly chopped

5 cloves garlic, crushed

1 fennel bulb, roughly chopped

1 onion, roughly chopped

1½ quarts water

1 tbsp. chopped basil

1 tbsp. chopped tarragon

Salt and freshly ground black pepper

Place all the ingredients except the herbs and water in a large pot and cook for 15 minutes over gentle heat. Add the water, which should cover the vegetables, and cook for a further 15 minutes. Remove from heat and add the herbs. Let stand for 5 minutes, then strain. Return the stock to the pot and boil until reduced by about half. Season lightly. Let it cool down, then refrigerate or freeze.

vinaigrettes

lemon grass vinaigrette

1 stalk lemon grass

⅔ cup olive oil

¼ cup tarragon vinegar

1 tsp. sugar

Salt and freshly ground black pepper

Serves 4

Bruise the lemongrass using a rolling pin or the bottom of a pan. Place the olive oil in a small pan with the lemon grass and heat through for 1 minute, then let it infuse for 15 minutes. Mix together the tarragon vinegar, sugar, salt, and pepper. Remove the lemongrass from the olive oil and discard. Gradually whisk the olive oil into the tarragon vinegar. Refrigerate until ready to use.

truffle vinaigrette

½ cup olive oil

2 tbsp. balsamic vinegar

1 tsp. sugar

1 tbsp. truffle trimmings

1 tsp. truffle oil

1 tomato, skinned, seeded, and finely diced

1 small bunch chives, finely chopped

Salt and freshly ground black pepper

Serves 4

Whisk the first 5 ingredients together in a bowl. Let stand for 2–3 hours to allow the flavors to develop. Just before serving, mix in the tomato and chives. Season, and serve immediately.

carrot and ginger vinaigrette

2 tbsp. olive oil

2 carrots, chopped

2 shallots, chopped

1-inch piece ginger root, peeled and finely chopped

Pat of butter

1 clove garlic, crushed

Pinch of saffron

1 sprig thyme

1 sprig rosemary

1 cup Chicken Stock

  (see page 153)

¼ cup heavy cream

Salt and freshly ground black pepper

Heat the olive oil in a pan over moderate heat. Add the carrots and shallots and sweat for 10 minutes. Add the ginger and butter. Cook gently, adding the garlic, saffron, and herbs. Season.

Add the stock, let it heat up, then simmer for 5–10 minutes. Stir in the cream, and let it cool. Blend in a food processor, then pass through a sieve into a clean pan. Reduce over medium heat until thick and creamy. Add seasoning. Reheat if necessary.

ginger and basil vinaigrette

½ cup olive oil

2 tbsp. balsamic vinegar

1 shallot, roughly chopped

1 clove garlic, crushed

1 tbsp. basil leaves

1-inch piece ginger root, peeled and finely chopped

1 tsp. warm water

1 egg yolk (optional)

Salt and freshly ground black pepper

Serves 4

Place all the ingredients in a blender or food processor and blend until smooth. Refrigerate until ready to use. Use within 24 hours.

champagne vinaigrette

½ cup olive oil

2 tbsp. good quality champagne vinegar

½ shallot, roughly chopped

½ tsp. sugar

Salt and freshly ground black pepper

To make the vinaigrette, place all the ingredients in a blender and process until smooth. Refrigerate until ready to use. Use within 3–4 days.

balsamic vinaigrette

½ cup olive oil

2 tbsp. good quality balsamic vinegar

½ shallot, roughly chopped

½ tsp. sugar

Salt and freshly ground black pepper

Place all the ingredients in a blender or food processor and blend until smooth. Refrigerate until ready to use. Use within 3–4 days.

walnut vinaigrette

1 tsp. Dijon mustard

2 tbsp. white wine vinegar

Salt and freshly ground black pepper

¼ cup walnut oil

¼ cup peanut oil

Whisk the mustard, vinegar, salt, and pepper together, then gradually whisk in the oils. Refrigerate until ready to use.

sauces and accompaniments

basil pesto

½ cup basil leaves

½ cup grated Parmesan

3 cloves garlic, chopped

1 tbsp. roasted pine nuts

2 tbsp. olive oil

Salt and freshly ground black pepper

Combine all dry ingredients in a food processor and slowly add the olive oil. Season well with salt and pepper. Store in a glass jar in the fridge for up to 1 week.

chile jam

½ cup white vinegar

6 tbsp. sugar

½ cup white wine

5oz. red chiles, seeded
  and roughly chopped

2 tbsp. butter

1 sprig thyme

Salt and freshly ground black pepper

Heat the vinegar and sugar in a pan until it has a syrup-like consistency. Bring to a boil and add the white wine. Return to a boil and add the chiles. Cook over high heat for 20 minutes, then add the butter and thyme. Blend in a food processor, season, and let it cool down.

oven-dried tomatoes

8 plum tomatoes, cut in half

Coarse salt

2 sprigs thyme

3 cloves garlic, sliced

3 tbsp. olive oil

Place the tomatoes in a roasting pan and sprinkle with the coarse salt, thyme, garlic, and olive oil. Place them in the oven at the lowest possible setting and let them dry out overnight.

onion and cilantro marmalade

2 tbsp. olive oil

8 red onions, finely sliced

½ stick (¼ cup) butter

Salt and freshly ground black pepper

½ cup sugar

1 sprig thyme

1 tbsp. red wine vinegar

½ cup grenadine

½ cup red wine

¼ cup Chicken Stock (see page 153)

1 cup cilantro, roughly chopped

Heat the olive oil in a large pan over medium heat and add the onions. Sauté for 2–3 minutes, then add the butter, salt, pepper, sugar, thyme, and vinegar. Cook for another 2–3 minutes until the butter has melted and the sugar has dissolved, then increase the heat and let it caramelize slightly. Add the grenadine, red wine, and stock. Continue to cook over high heat until the liquid has reduced and the onions have a jam-like consistency. Add the cilantro, adjust the seasoning, and let it cool.

sun-dried tomato tapenade

8oz. sundried tomatoes in oil, drained (about 1⅓ cups)

⅓ cup pitted black olives

1 small bunch chives, roughly chopped

1 tbsp. chopped parsley

1 tbsp. chopped cilantro

4 cloves garlic, roughly chopped

1 tbsp. anchovy paste

¼ cup olive oil

Salt and freshly ground black pepper

Blend all the ingredients together in a food processor until the texture is very fine. Press through a fine sieve, using the back of a wooden spoon. Adjust the seasoning if necessary and serve.
To store, spoon into a jar, top up with olive oil, and keep sealed.

garlic cream

4 cloves garlic, very finely crushed

1 cup heavy cream

½ cup Chicken Stock (see page 153)

1 sprig rosemary

1 sprig thyme

Place all ingredients together in a small pan and boil rapidly until reduced by a quarter. Strain and reheat if necessary.

red pepper coulis

1stick (½ cup) butter

4 red bell peppers, seeded and diced

4 shallots, diced

1 leek, white part only, diced

1 celery stalk, diced

2 cloves garlic, crushed

1 sprig thyme

1 bay leaf

Salt and freshly ground black pepper

Sugar

2 cups tomato juice

Melt the butter in a pan over moderate heat and add the vegetables, garlic and herbs. Cook gently until tender. Season and add sugar to taste. Add the tomato juice and simmer until the peppers are tender. Blend in a food processor then press through a fine sieve. Season, and add water if necessary to give a pouring consistency.

watercress purée

2 tbsp. butter

2 cups watercress

2 pints heavy cream

Salt and freshly ground black pepper

Melt the butter in a pan over medium heat and sauté the watercress until tender. Add enough of the cream to cover. Blend until smooth in a food processor, then press through a fine sieve and return to a clean pan. Add more cream, season, and reduce slightly.

parmesan cream

4 egg yolks

2½ cups olive oil

1 cup peanut oil

3½ cups grated Parmesan

3 shallots, finely diced

2 cloves garlic, crushed

1 sprig thyme, leaves removed

2 tbsp. champagne vinegar

Salt and freshly ground black pepper

In a food processor, blend the egg yolks and oil until it is the consistency of mayonnaise. Add the Parmesan, shallots, garlic, and thyme. Blend again until the texture is smooth. Add the vinegar, salt, and pepper.

crayfish sauce

1lb. saltwater crayfish shells

1 carrot, chopped

1 Spanish onion, chopped

4 shallots, chopped

1 head garlic

½ fennel bulb, chopped

1 small red chile, seeded

6 vine tomatoes

2 tbsp. Tomato Fondue (see page 157)

½ tbsp. chopped parsley

½ cup dry vermouth

½ cup brandy

½ cup white wine

1 cup fish stock

1¾ cups heavy cream

Place the crayfish shells in a wide pan and roast over high heat for about 5 minutes. Add the carrot, onion, shallots, garlic, fennel, chile, tomatoes, and tomato fondue, and let it caramelize for about 5 minutes. Add the vermouth and brandy, and heat for 2–3 minutes to drive off the alcohol. Add the white wine and fish stock. Simmer gently for about 2 hours over low heat. Strain through a fine sieve, return to a clean pan, and heat until reduced to 2 cups. Add the cream and simmer gently for about 5 minutes.

tomato sauce

Olive oil

8 plum tomatoes

2 cloves garlic, crushed

4 shallots, diced

Sprig of thyme

Sprig of rosemary

1 red bell pepper, seeded and diced

1 red chile, seeded and diced

2 tbsp. Tomato Fondue (see page 157)

½ vanilla bean

Salt and freshly ground black pepper

2½ cups Chicken Stock (see page 153)

Heat the olive oil in a medium-sized pan over medium heat. Slowly add the tomatoes, garlic, shallots, thyme, rosemary, pepper, chile, tomato fondue, and vanilla bean. Stir gently, season, and add the chicken stock. Simmer gently for 20 minutes and strain through a fine sieve.

mushroom sauce

½lb. white mushrooms

2 cloves garlic, diced

1 sprig thyme

8 shallots, diced

1 carrot, finely diced

1 leek (white part only), diced

Lemon zest

Orange zest

1 vanilla bean

¾ cup plus 2 tbsp. sugar

1 red bell pepper, seeded and diced

2 cups balsamic vinegar

1¼ cups Chicken Stock (see page 153)

Place all ingredients in a large casserole dish over moderate heat. Simmer until reduced by half. Strain the sauce through a fine sieve.

pesto couscous

2 tbsp. butter

10oz. (1⅔ cups) couscous

1¼ cups Chicken or Vegetable Stock (see page 153)

¼ cup Basil Pesto (see page 155)

Juice of 2 lemons

Melt the butter in a medium-sized pan over gentle heat. Add the couscous and cook for 1 minute, stirring. In a separate pan, heat the stock to boiling point, and then stir it into the couscous. Stir in the pesto and lemon juice.

goat cheese cream

14oz. soft goat cheese

2 tomatoes, roughly chopped

3 tbsp. chopped basil

Freshly ground black pepper

1–2 tbsp. heavy cream

Mix all the ingredients together to make a smooth paste. Add more cream if you want to thin out the consistency. Use on canapés.

pepper stew

4 shallots, finely diced

2 cloves garlic, crushed and finely diced

1 red onion, finely diced

1 green bell pepper, seeded and finely diced

1 yellow bell pepper, seeded and finely diced

1 red bell pepper, seeded and finely diced

1 sprig thyme, leaves removed

2 tbsp. Tomato Fondue (see right)

Sauté the shallots, garlic, and red onion in a hot frying pan for 1 minute. Add the peppers and thyme, and cook for 5–6 minutes. Let them cool down, then stir in the tomato fondue.

garlic confit

Using the duck or goose fat will give a better flavor.

16 cloves garlic, unpeeled

Vegetable oil, duck fat or goose fat

1 bay leaf

1 sprig rosemary

1 sprig thyme

4 black peppercorns

Bring a small pan of water to a boil and blanch the garlic for 1 minute. Remove the garlic with a slotted spoon, refresh it under cold running water, then return it to the pan. Repeat the blanching and refreshing twice more.

Meanwhile, heat the oil or fat in a small pan to about 195°F. Add the garlic and the remaining ingredients, and cook at 175°F for about 10 minutes. The garlic should be tender, but not too colored. Drain on paper towels and serve immediately, or let it cool in the fat and keep it in the fridge for up to 1 week.

tomato fondue

1 tablespoon olive oil

4 shallots, finely chopped

2 cloves garlic, crushed

8 plum tomatoes, skinned, seeded, and chopped

1 sprig thyme

1 sprig rosemary

1 tablespoon tomato paste

Salt and freshly ground black pepper

Heat the oil in a pan over a medium heat and sweat the shallots and garlic until soft but not colored. Add the tomatoes, herbs, and tomato paste. Simmer gently until the liquid has all evaporated and the mixture is quite dry. Season well and let it cool. Refrigerate until ready to use.

beef jus

3 cups Beef Stock (see page 153)

¾ stick (⅓ cup) butter

2 tbsp. olive oil

Bring the beef stock to a boil in a large pan, then simmer until reduced by one-third. Whisk in the butter and olive oil and adjust the seasoning.

basil bread

3lbs. (about 12 cups) white bread flour

2oz. yeast

3 tbsp. salt

4 tbsp chopped basil

2 cups warm water

Mix all of the ingredients together. Let the dough rise for one hour. Bake in a preheated oven at 425°F for 50 minutes.

pasta dough

4 cups white bread flour

6 egg yolks

4 eggs

2 tbsp. olive oil

1 tbsp. salt

Mix all of the ingredients together to form a dough. Set it aside for one hour, then cut it with a pasta machine.

index

acknowledgements

The publisher would like to thank the following for their kind assistance in lending props for photoshoots: Nicole Farhi, Mint, The Conran Shop, and Divertimenti.